# Productive Spindling

## Spindle Spinning in the Early 21$^{st}$ Century

from Ask The Bellwether

by Amelia Garripoli

to Natalie Carlson and Nikolai Carlson. The day will come when you will have spun, knit, and woven for longer than your mother.

# Productive Spindling

Copyright © 2009 by Amelia Garripoli

All rights reserved. No portion of this book may be reproduced or utilized in any form, or by any electronic, mechanical, or other means without the prior written permission of the author or publisher.

Portions of this work appeared previously in Spindling: The Basics, by the same author.

Photograph copyrights held by their photographer, used with permission.

Printed in the United States of America by Brisk Printing.

ISBN-13: 978-0-9824381-0-7
ISBN-10: 0-98234381-0-9
Library of Congress Cataloging in Publication Data Pending

Published by
Ask The Bellwether
3329 Upland Lane
Port Angeles WA 98362

askthebellwether.blogspot.com
ameliastwist@gmail.com

Distributed by The Bellwether
www.thebellwether.com
ask@thebellwether.com

9 8 7 6 5 4 3 1 0

Cover design by Melanie Reed, photo by Natalie Carlson, spindle-spun yarn and items by Amelia Garripoli
Interior photos by Amelia Garripoli, Natalie Carlson, Nikolai Carlson, and friends from Ravelry – please see Accolades and Credits for the full list
Drawings by Amelia Garripoli

# PRODUCTIVE SPINDLING

## Contents

Part One ...................................................................................1

**Spindling, The Basics** ............................................................2

    Choosing Your First Spindle..................................... 2

    Choosing Your First Fiber ......................................... 3

    Drafting Fiber: An Experiment.................................. 4

    Learning with a Leader ............................................. 5

    Your First Singles ...................................................... 6

    Your First Plying........................................................ 8

    Finishing Your First Skein ......................................... 9

**Part Two** ...............................................................................11

**Spindle Choice** .....................................................................12

    Spindle Type ............................................................ 12

    Notched or Not?...................................................... 12

    Hook ........................................................................ 13

    Shaft Length............................................................ 14

    Shaft Diameter ........................................................ 14

    Wobble .................................................................... 15

    Whorl Diameter....................................................... 15

    Whorl Shape ............................................................ 16

    Spindle Weight ........................................................ 16

    Plying Spindle Choice .............................................. 17

**Productively Filling a Spindle**...............................................18

    An Efficient Leader .................................................. 18

    Thigh Roll and the Bottom Whorl .......................... 19

    Bottom-Whorl Half-Hitch ....................................... 19

    Bottom-Whorl Leader ............................................. 20

    Efficient Wind-On .................................................... 20

    Bottom-Whorl Cop Building .................................... 22

    Bottom-Whorl Turkish Spindles.............................. 22

Efficient Drafting.................................................................23

    Worsted Drafting.........................................................23

    Woolen Drafting .........................................................24

    Long-Staple Drafting ..................................................24

    Short-Staple Drafting .................................................25

How Full Can You Fill A Spindle? .........................................25

Rate of Spindling.................................................................26

Balanced Cop .....................................................................27

Drafting Singles on Full Spindles..........................................27

Finding More Time to Spindle .............................................27

Putting the Spindle Down ....................................................28

Managing Fiber...................................................................28

Consistency of Spinning.......................................................29

Join Techniques ..................................................................30

Maximize Productivity .........................................................31

Spin Direction ....................................................................32

## Productive Plying...............................................................33

Plying Technique.................................................................34

Andean Plying Bracelet........................................................36

Beauty-wave Plying Bracelet ................................................36

Consistency in Plying ..........................................................37

Broken Singles When Plying .................................................38

Yarn Improvements .............................................................39

Navajo Ply .........................................................................39

A Full Spindle! ....................................................................40

## General Tips .....................................................................42

Transportability ..................................................................42

Useful Tools .......................................................................42

If you also Spin on a Wheel ... .............................................43

Spindling and Walking .........................................................43

Using Your Handspun ..........................................................44

## Spindler's Bibliography .........................................................46

## Accolades and Credits ..........................................................48

## Index ...............................................................................49

# PRODUCTIVE SPINDLING

## Part One

Have you walked away from your spindles in frustration? Do you want to expand your repertoire from wheel to spindle so you can bring spinning on your travels? Are you sure there must be some way to make spindling more productive?

Let's explore all this and more — we'll find what spindle features provides the best spin, how to use the features your spindle has to the best result, and cover a variety of top-whorl methods, bottom-whorl methods, and generally handy techniques to get more out of your spindling.

If you are new to spindling, start with Part One: Spindling, The Basics. Experienced spindlers may find a few nuggets in the basics too. We'll expand on many topics and present more techniques in Part Two of **Productive Spindling**.

Fiber, Bosworth spindle, and skein of singles (photo by ellenspn)

# Spindling, The Basics

Spindling has been around since people began weaving cloth. Before the fifteenth century, spindling or one of its precursors was the only way to make yarn and thread. All of those fine Egyptian mummy-wrappings? Spindle-spun. Sails for ships? Spindle-spun. It's been discovered that there were once breeds of sheep with far finer wool than today's Merino, the finest wool known today. Today, spindling is a great hobby, craft, and art for those wanting to make beautiful yarn in this peaceful, portable way.

When you are learning to spin, break up your spinning time across several days. It takes your muscles and your head time to absorb what they learn and develop the new skills. You will be surprised how much a night's sleep improves your spindling! Each skill can take several sessions to learn, and the combination of all of them takes practice to coordinate and control. Give yourself time to learn and enjoy your new skill.

## Choosing Your First Spindle

There are several kinds of spindles available to the spindler today, each with its benefits and abilities. Let's start with a top-whorl spindle, also called the high-whorl spindle. These are readily available in a wide range of weights and can also be inexpensively constructed.

A top-whorl spindle consists of a shaft: the long, rod part; a whorl: the wheel-like part; and a hook. The whorl is near the top of the shaft and the hook is attached to the top of the shaft.

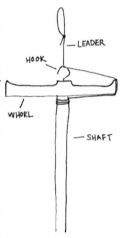

The longer spinning spindles have more weight out at the rim of the whorl than in the center, and a relatively thin shaft. The diameter of the whorl and the weight of the spindle will affect how thickly or thinly the wool can be spun. The whorl and shaft need to be balanced for the spindle to spin without wobbling. There are other factors that cause a spindle to wobble as well, such as hook placement and distribution of yarn on the shaft. We'll return to that later.

A good size of spindle whorl to start with is two to three inches (5-7.5 cm) across. The larger the whorl is, the longer the spindle will spin. The smaller the whorl is, the shorter the spindle will spin, because it concentrates weight near the shaft, making the spindle spin for a shorter time. Weight near the shaft will also make the spindle more stable, reducing any wobble from an unevenly built-up cop.

You can combine these two spinning behaviors with a wide whorl that is dished out mid-way between the rim and the shaft – this makes a spindle that can spin for a long time with minimal wobble.

A good shaft length to start with is nine to twelve inches (22-30 cm), depending on the whorl diameter. The shaft adds to the weight of the spindle and helps balance the whorl. It needs to be long enough to store your yarn and have room for your fingers to spin the spindle.

A good weight for a spindle to learn with is anything from 1.5 to 2.2 ounces (40-60 grams). Much heavier, and it is a 'boat anchor', which can be difficult to spin well unless you are plying or spinning very thickly. Much lighter, and it has a tendency to lose its spin very rapidly when you are first learning. You may find that as your skills improve, you like a slightly lighter spindle for a greater range of yarn thickness. Your first spindle, however, can still be a useful plying spindle. We'll discuss spindle weights more in Part Two.

Whether you start with bottom-whorl or top-whorl is up to you. Some say that a bottom-whorl spindle is easier to control, but I found that my top-whorl spindle could use the same techniques, and then I could advance to the super-fast thigh rolling that the top-whorl spindle is famous for. These basic instructions focus on using a top-whorl spindle. We'll discuss bottom-whorl methods – and even thigh rolling bottom whorls, later.

## Choosing Your First Fiber

When learning to spin, it is easiest to start with wool that has been processed into roving. You can start with raw fleece, but then you either need a prime fleece that can be spun in the grease, or you will need to wash and card the fleece before spinning it. One thing at a time, start with roving for learning to spin, and learn fiber preparation techniques later.

Roving is wool that has been washed and carded into a long, continuous tube of unspun fiber It can be anything from pencil roving, which is about as thick as a pencil, to a fat roving that is as thick as your arm. Commercial top is also very widely available; it can be a bit tricky to learn on, being more compacted than roving – but if you find some you like, try it. Liking your first fiber goes a long way toward your enjoyment of the learning process.

Wool is classified several different ways: sheep breeds, how finely it can be spun, or the diameter of the individual fibers. This last one has convenient categories to start with – fine, medium, and coarse. It is easiest to learn with medium or medium-fine wool such as Romney, Corriedale, or Blue Faced Leicester.

Look for roving that will interest you, from white or natural colors, to a multi-color dyed roving. Expect to use one-half to one pound of fiber as you learn to spin. Your roving should be well-prepared, open but not fly-away. It should not be matted, felted, or sticky. Hold a length in your hands with your hands eight to twelve inches apart. You should be able to easily pull it an inch or so longer without it falling apart and without undue tugging. This gentle pull is called *drafting*.

Angora, mohair, silk, alpaca, cashmere and other fibers present their own challenges. You'll have plenty to learn when starting to spin; save the exotics for later. For now, find a wool roving you like to hold in your hands. If you don't like the feel of it or the color isn't appealing, then you won't enjoy spinning it and won't want to practice with it. You *will* get some fun, usable yarn from this – although it's best not to start out planning to knit a sweater for your mother-in-law's birthday next week.

Even roving may have vegetable matter (VM) in it. These seeds, hay, or grass pieces show that your fiber came from a living, eating animal and was not heavily processed with chemicals. When you come to some VM in spinning, stop if you need to, and pick it out. It will not wash out of the finished yarn, and will leave harsh spots if left in.

Remember your fiber's staple length; we'll use it again later.

Gently pull a few fibers out of one end of your roving, and determine your *staple length* – this is the average length of the fibers in the roving, and is usually between three and seven inches. Take a close look at the fibers for *crimp*, or waviness, of the wool, and the *diameter* of the individual wool fibers. Medium grade wool has a diameter of 22-31 microns – no, I don't expect you to be able to measure the diameter! Crimp is a 'good thing': it helps the fiber stay together when it is spun. It can help guide how fine you spin the fiber, and how many twists per inch to put in it – but that comes later, don't worry about that for now.

## Drafting Fiber: An Experiment

I will state up front: these instructions are how I teach spindling. Yes, I'm right-handed. However, lefties may find they have an advantage using this method, as the hand holding the fiber (and, actually, in control) is the left hand. Once we get past a few basic steps, I'll get more generic in my handedness descriptions, but for now, stick with me. Spindlers teach both of their hands to be dexterous, so we may as well use both from the start.

Start without the spindle, drafting fiber and twisting it on your thigh. Separate a six- to twelve-inch-long piece of your roving from the rest by holding the roving about four inches from the end and gently pulling that hand away from the rest of the roving. This should give you a piece six- to twelve-inches long, for this first step.

*Pre-drafting* is useful for improving compacted roving, roving that won't draft freely, or to thin very wide roving. Take your length of roving, divide it lengthwise until it is about as thick as your thumb, and give it a few good shakes from each end to help open it up. If it is still not drafting freely, hold your hands about 1.5 staple lengths apart and pull gently until the fibers just barely begin to slide. Repeat this pull along the length of the piece to help it open up.

Hold the piece of roving in your left hand. With your right hand, draft, or gently pull, a small amount of fiber from the end without pulling it completely apart from the rest of the piece. Lay it on your right thigh under your hand, and roll it up your leg toward your stomach using the fingers of your right hand. As the twist approaches the undrafted part of the roving, gently draft out a little more fiber by pulling away slowly with your left hand.

The amount of fiber you draft out of the roving before spinning controls the thickness of your yarn. If you draft only a few fibers, you will have thin yarn. If you draft more fibers, you will have thicker yarn.

If your fiber will not draft, make sure your hands are more than a staple length apart; if your hands are far enough apart, then you may need to loosen up your fiber with more pre-drafting.

Once you have twist in a foot or so of the drafted and rolled roving, hold the ends of the twisted portion so as not to let the twist escape, and pull it off of the rest of the roving. Fold this spun part in half, pinch the ends in one hand, and let it twist on itself along its length. Yes, it's yarn!

This twisting is called *plying*, which stabilizes the yarn — if you let go, it won't untwist. We'll cover plying later.

You can play with the drafting and the amount of twist you put into the yarn to see how it affects the yarn thickness, the puffiness or tightness of the plied yarn, and the ease of drafting.

The size of your yarn is determined by how much fiber is caught by the twist as it is drafted. If a lot of fiber is caught, you get thick yarn. If less fiber is caught, you get thin yarn. When spinning, your goal is to pay attention to the fiber which is between your hands and control how much becomes yarn.

If you look closely at your yarn before you fold it, you will see that the fiber has an angle in it. This is Z twist. Note that the angle of twist in the yarn matches the middle bar of the Z, that is, it is a right-slanting angle.

## Learning with a Leader

Take a two-foot length of yarn and make a *leader*. You will attach your roving to this leader to start spindling on an empty spindle. Make a slip-knot in one end and put it on the shaft, just under the whorl. Make a loop on the other end with an overhand knot.

It is best to use a plied yarn for your leader, so when you start to spin it can take up some of the initial twist from the spinning before you draft. Yes, you can use commercial yarn, cotton, acrylic, any fiber you like.

You can spin without a leader – but we want to learn a few things first, so let's start with a leader and move on to spindling without a leader later.

We need to digress about handedness briefly. Right-handed? Then your left hand is your *fiber hand*, holding the fiber supply you are spinning, and your right hand is your *spindle hand*, twirling the spindle and then coming up to draft fiber from your fiber hand. Left-handed? Then your right hand is your *fiber hand*, holding the fiber supply you are spinning, and your left hand is your *spindle hand*, twirling the spindle and then coming up to draft fiber from your fiber hand.

That said, when I say clockwise, I mean clockwise – right- or left-handed, that direction of twist doesn't change. And, if you find your "handedness" assignments are not working for you – sure, try the others. It's not set in stone.

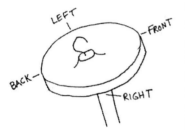

Wrap the leader a few times around the shaft at the whorl clockwise; then bring it out, around the whorl, and up to the hook at the top of the spindle. If there is a notch in the whorl, run the yarn through the notch before bringing it through the hook. You will find once you start to spin that a notch to the right of the hook or directly behind the hook is best for spinning clockwise, and to the left of the hook or directly behind for counter-clockwise. Right and left are determined by looking down on the hook with the open end facing away from you.

Ready to spin on your spindle? Hold the end of the leader in your fiber hand. Give the spindle a clockwise spin with your spindle hand by flicking the lower end of the shaft between your thumb and index finger. A clockwise spin is used to making singles with Z twist as we did earlier. See how long the spindle spins. Once it slows, give it another spin. Let it slow to a stop and see how it reverses direction, untwisting the leader.

How quickly twist enters the leader is related to how quickly the spindle rotates. Once the leader has a lot of twist in it, the spindle is quick to slow and reverse direction.

If the spindle wobbles, check for these causes:

Check your hand placement when twisting the spindle. Are you moving the shaft so that it is not vertical, at the start or completion of your hand-twirl of the spindle?

Is the whorl perpendicular to the shaft? If not, see if it can be shifted to make it perpendicular. This is possible with spindles that do not have the whorl glued to the shaft, such as CD spindles.

Does the yarn line up with the center of the shaft? If the whorl has no notch, then try running the yarn up from the side, rather than from behind, the hook. As a last resort, gently bend the hook – just a little – to let the yarn go up as if continuing the center line of the shaft.

## Your First Singles

Now we put together drafting and spinning the spindle. Take a piece of roving as before, and draft out from the end of your piece of fiber a piece no thicker than your little finger, that is as long as the staple length of the fiber. Keeping it attached to the piece of roving, place half the length of this drafted part through the loop on the spindle's leader and fold it back on itself, pinching both sides with your fiber hand. Hold the spindle in your spindle hand.

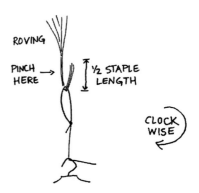

Give the spindle a clockwise spin with your spindle hand. Once you feel twist in the pinched fiber and see twist in the leader, stop the spindle and put ('park') the shaft between your knees. Pinch with your spindle hand right below your fiber hand's pinch, effectively transferring the pinch to your spindle hand. Move your fiber hand up the fiber and draft back like you did when pre-drafting, this time moving the roving up, away from the spindle. You are tugging against the pinch your spindle hand has on the fiber, so be sure to hang on with that hand. How thinly you draft out your fiber controls how thick your yarn will be.

Next, slide your spindle hand's pinch slowly up the drafted fiber — the twist will follow it up, creating yarn. You have yarn if tugging on the length no longer drafts it longer. If it still lengthens, it needs more twist to be yarn. If it is really highly twisted, draft out more until there are no corkscrews in the yarn. If the twist slows or does not follow, then re-pinch with your fiber hand at the end of the twisted section just above your spindle hand's pinch, and spin the spindle again to put more twist in the yarn. Continue with spinning, parking, and drafting until you have an arm's length of singles.

Once you have an arm's length, you need to wind this new yarn onto the spindle. With your fiber hand pinching between the yarn and the unspun fiber, and your spindle hand holding the spindle, hold the yarn taut so it does not twist on itself. Moving your spindle hand and the spindle, unhook the leader from the hook, wind the leader and the newly spun length of yarn onto the spindle shaft, and re-thread the yarn around the whorl and through the hook, with four to six inches of spun singles above the hook. This length will store the twist for your next draft.

Then you begin again. Your fiber hand will hold the roving, keeping the twist from entering the fiber before you want it to; it will also draft out fiber against the pinch of your spindle hand to prepare it to become yarn. Your spindle hand will twirl the spindle and control the release of the twist into the drafted fiber. Once you have a new length, wind it onto the spindle. This four-step process – spin, park, draft, wind-on – is often referred to as *park & draft*.

Now is a good time to take a break. You'll want to get comfortable with the motions of spin-park-draft-wind-on, so repeat this process for a few sessions.

Once you are comfortable with park & draft, it's time to combine these into one continuous step, and draft while spinning. Take your partially full spindle, pre-draft out a staple length or two of fiber above the yarn, and pinch below that pre-drafted length. Have about six inches of yarn above the hook, not wound onto the spindle yet. Pre-drafting and the extra length of yarn above the hook will give you time to move your hands. You will slide up the pre-drafted area without having to spend thought or time drafting it out, and then start drafting again once you are above it.

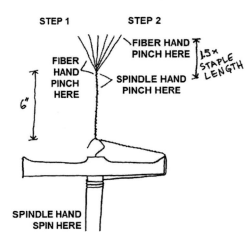

Step 1: Hold the roving in the palm of your fiber hand and with that hand, pinch the fiber at the location where the twist stops – the boundary between yarn and roving. With your spindle hand, twirl the spindle to start it spinning.

Step 2: Move your spindle hand up to pinch just below your fiber hand. Move your fiber hand up the fiber supply, to be 1.5 times the staple length above the spindle hand.

Now with your spindle hand, draft some fiber down from the roving. Then quickly slide your right hand up the newly drafted fiber and pinch again just above the new yarn. The twist will just as quickly follow your right hand up the fiber, turning it into yarn. Move your fiber hand up so it remains 1.5 staple lengths above your spindle hand.

Repeat this draft-slide-pinch motion with your spindle hand and your fiber hand, maintaining the distance between them, until your spindle slows or stops.

When your spindle slows or stops, move your fiber hand to pinch the roving where the twist stops entering it, and start the spindle again with your spindle hand. Then continue with the motions described above.

When the spindle is about to touch the ground or you have a long-enough length of yarn, wind the new yarn onto the cop of yarn forming on the spindle shaft under the whorl, then begin again.

This is a lot to coordinate, isn't it? It can be difficult to move your hands quickly enough, or to get them in the right spots. The spindle may stop or reverse direction when you are looking at the fiber. You might want to go back to park & draft and see how your left and right hands coordinate, then try this again. Take a break, too.

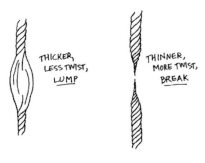

Your yarn may be thick and thin as you learn to draft and to handle the spindle speed. Once you can spin and draft at the same time, don't hesitate to do one or the other alone. Over-twisted fiber can be untwisted by letting the spindle spin the other way briefly. Thick spots can be untwisted and drafted thinner, and then re-twisted. Under-twisted spots can have more twist put in. Look over each length of new yarn to see if you'd like to alter it before winding it on the spindle.

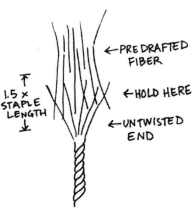

At some point, your fiber will separate when being drafted, your yarn will break at a thin or overspun spot, or you'll reach the end of your piece of fiber. You *join* fiber to the end of your spun yarn to continue spinning. The key to a successful join is to have the two ends being joined be entirely unspun, at least as long as 1.5 times the fiber's staple length, and have the two ends not be overly thin, so that they can be drafted together. If the break was at a thin spot, find a thicker spot further up the yarn, untwist a portion between your hands, and pull it apart there. Use this as the new end to join to your roving. Have a 1.5-times-staple-length-long piece of unspun fiber pre-drafted from the roving and prepare an unspun length from the end of the yarn by untwisting it with your fingers.

Fan the fibers of both ends out and lay one on top of the other. Put your spindle in your lap and with both hands, draft them together to start the fibers intermingling and make the desired thickness of yarn. Pinch at the base of the

**The Basics ● 7**

join near the yarn with your fiber hand, and spin the spindle. Once there is some extra twist in the yarn ready to move up into the join area, slowly slide your fingers up the join to let twist into the join. Once past the join, continue drafting between fiber hand and spindle hand as before.

It can take a few tries to get a good join. If your first try doesn't work, find another good spot, look for one that's a bit thick, in the yarn to use.

Your spindle is full when it won't hold any more yarn. Sometimes, you run out of room under the whorl. More often, the yarn won't stay in the hook or slips around the whorl. These are all indications that the spindle cannot hold more yarn. In this case, it is time to ply or finish your yarn.

To get more speed, you can use the technique that the top-whorl spindle is renowned for. Instead of starting the twist with your fingers, roll the spindle clockwise with the flat of your spindle hand against your thigh. Right-handed? Clockwise roll is from knee to hip on your right thigh. Left-handed? Clockwise roll is from hip to knee on your left thigh.

Use the thigh roll to start the spindle spinning and see how fast it can go!

## Your First Plying

Once you have singles, you can stop there, or ply. On a spindle, the easiest way to ply is either to make an Andean plying bracelet or a center-pull ball. Commercial ball winders are readily available in yarn shops, or traditional nostepinnes can be used to wind center-pull balls. We'll cover Andean plying later.

Make a center-pull ball with your singles. Then take both ends and wind a new, two-strand center-pull ball. This is easiest to do if you hold the first center-pull ball on your thumb while winding the two-strand ball, so that you can keep the outer strand under control and maintain even tension on both the inner and outer strands. Tuck the outer end under the outermost wraps so it won't fly off the final center-pull ball.

If you do not have a ball winder, rewind your spindleful of yarn onto a cardboard tube such as a paper towel core, catching the start of the end in a slit you've cut on the tube. When done, slide the wound yarn onto your thumb, take the inner and outer ends, and wind both strands together onto your cardboard tube again, to make a two-strand ball you can pull from the center or the outside.

Attach a leader to your spindle as above, but now wind it on counter-clockwise. Take the inside two strands of your center-pull ball and attach them to the loop at the top of the leader. Pull them through the loop so there's a three-inch length, then wind that length back around and through the loop again, to hold it fairly firmly.

Plying is done by spinning the spindle counter-clockwise, to introduce an S twist. Ply yarn to balance the singles' Z twist so that you have a balanced yarn. It is best to test freshly spun singles to see how much plying they need. To do this, take a six inch length of freshly spun single, fold it in half, and let it twist on itself. The result shows you how much twist you need to have balanced plied yarn. I do this *plyback test* continuously while spinning singles to ensure even twist throughout the spindleful, matching each length of new yarn to a sample of balanced yarn saved from the start of the spinning. Match the sample when plying as well for a consistent yarn.

plyback test

Position your hands as for spinning singles, but spin the spindle counter-clockwise. At the start, keep both the end through the loop and the two strands pinched together, until all four strands are plied together – like when we spun the first folded-through tuft of yarn into our initial inches of singles. Once this initial length is plied, slide back and let twist enter the un-plied portions. You can draft from the center-pull ball much more quickly than from the roving, since you do not need to worry about how much fiber is coming out or the fiber separating. If the singles are kinked, you may need to stop and straighten them out so that two smooth singles enter the twist area and are smoothly plied.

Look closely at the resulting plied yarn. You will see that the angle of the twist is the reverse of the singles. It is called S twist: the angle matches the middle bar of the S, that is, it is a left-slanting angle.

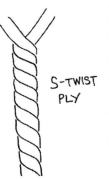
S-TWIST PLY

When you get an arm's length, stop and wind it onto the shaft counter-clockwise. Continue with this until you have plied the entire ball.

As with singles, you can use the thigh roll to get more speed. Remember, for plying, the spindle needs to spin counter-clockwise. Right-handed? When plying, roll from hip to knee on your right leg. Left-handed? When plying, roll from knee to hip on your left leg.

You can do three or more plies by taking multiple spindles of yarn and plying them together. There are devices available that will hold spindles to ply from, such as the Lizzy Kate from Greensleeves. Or, you can wind a multi-strand ball to ply from using several spindlefuls of singles. We'll cover more plying methods later.

## Finishing Your First Skein

Starting a niddy-noddy

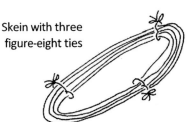

Skein with three figure-eight ties

Congratulations on your new yarn! Once you have your spindle of singles or plied yarn, you will want to wind it off into a skein. If you have a niddy-noddy, wind it on that. See the picture for a guide to winding on the niddy-noddy. While the yarn is still on the niddy-noddy, tie the skein in at least three places with lengths of yarn and then remove it from the niddy-noddy.

If you do not have a niddy-noddy, hold your fiber arm at a right angle, and wind the yarn in a circle starting in the angle between your thumb and fingers, around and under your arm above your elbow, then back around the other side and up to the angle between your thumb and fingers again. When you have your skein, carefully remove it from your arm, and tie the skein in at least three places with lengths of yarn.

To finish the yarn, you need to wash it. This sets the twist and cleans the yarn. Wool yarn may shrink in length and get puffier. To wash, fill your sink with warm water and some wool wash and then gently place the skein in the water and press to submerge it. You do not want to run water directly onto the skein or agitate the skein in the water, as that may cause it to felt. Let it sit in the soapy water for ten minutes. Remove it, drain the water. If the water is very dirty, repeat this. Keep the water at the same temperature each time, as a change in temperature may cause the yarn to felt. Repeat this process without the wool wash to rinse the yarn; one or two rinses may be needed. Remember, do not agitate the yarn or fill the sink with the yarn in it. You can gently squeeze the skein while it is in the water to help the soap wash it or to help rinse it. Once the skein is washed, roll it in a towel and gently squeeze it; do not wring it. Let the skein dry on a towel or rack.

If you are planning to weave with your skein, it should be dried with weights; hang the skein from a hanger, and put a weight at the bottom of the skein to make it taut. Yarn that will be used for knitting or crochet will be loftier if it is not weighted when it is drying.

**The BASICS ● 9**

If your yarn looks kinky after you wash it, you can smooth it out with steam. Pass the skein over the spout of a steaming teakettle; five to ten seconds is enough to smooth most yarns.

If you set the twist without weights, you can tell if your yarn is balanced by hanging the dried skein. If the skein does not twist or only twists up to two complete revolutions, it is balanced. If the entire skein twists S, then either the singles were overspun (overplied) for the amount of ply or not enough twist was put in the ply. If the entire skein twists Z, then either the singles were underspun (underplied) for the amount of ply, or too much twist was put into the ply. Unbalanced yarn is usable. If you plan to knit with it, knit a sample first to see if there is any bias in the stitches. Garter stitch may produce an even result even if stockinette stitch biases.

Once your skein is dry, you can twist it up into a traditional skein shape. Hold the skein at both ends and twist, as shown in the first picture. Then, fold it in half and it will twist back on itself; place one end through the opening of the other end.

Congratulations on learning to spin! Enjoy your first skein — it is unique yarn. It is likely that there is a spinning guild in your area, and there are many internet communities involved in spindling. Bring your first skein, your questions, and your interest — welcome!

Learning to spindle - first skein (photo by riverpoet)

# PRODUCTIVE SPINDLING

## Part Two

We're on our way now that the basics are covered. Let's dive into more advanced spindling techniques, with a focus on productivity.

Starting with spindle features, we'll find what provides the best spin, how to use the features your spindle has to the best result, and cover a variety of top-whorl methods, bottom-whorl methods, and generally handy techniques to get more out of your spindling. Drafting methods tailored to your fiber, and choosing fibers are discussed. We'll wrap up with finishing yarn and spinning yarn for a purpose.

Silk spun on a Golding spindle (photo by sherie)

# Spindle Choice

Spindle dynamics drive your productivity. Let's start by looking at the type, parts, shape and mass of your spindle as they affect your spindling.

## Spindle Type

There is a wide variety of spindles from a wide variety of cultures; in this book, top-whorl and bottom-whorl spindles are the focus, as they are the most efficient spindles. Any spindle can be used efficiently, given enough practice and study of the actions used.

Top-whorl spindles have a hook at the top, the whorl near the hooked end, and the shaft extends below the whorl. Bottom-whorl spindles have a hook or an indentation at the top, the shaft going down, and the whorl placed at the far end of the shaft.

The methods used here apply to both top whorls and bottom whorls; I will try to be clear when there are specific differences, and admit to having filled more top-whorl spindles than bottom-whorl spindles, though I use both.

## Notched or Not?

If the spindle is notched, then your yarn is less likely to slip around the whorl once the yarn on the spindle, called the *cop*, has reached a diameter close to the whorl's diameter. This slipping can still happen with notched spindles, so consider notch depth as well.

Notches can be placed anywhere on the whorl relative to the opening of the hook. Some hooks do better with notches to the left and right of the opening, some with one notch at the back of the hook. Some whorl shapes may offer you several options for stable yarn placement — a square whorl has no notch, as yarn brought up on the middle of an edge does not tend to slip forward or back.

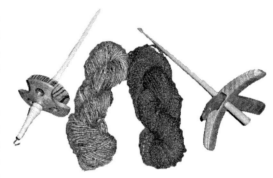

The Forrester Dervish has a hook at the top of its shaft. The Jenkins Turkish has an indent near the top of its shaft. Left skein: thick singles; right skein: cabled merino.

Kundert has a notch at 3 o'clock (photo by stringplayer). Bosworth has a notch at 6 o'clock. Spindlewood's square acts like a notch on each side (photo by marihana).

You can create a virtual notch yourself, as shown in the picture series below. ❶Start spindling by putting the hook into the tuft of fiber at the end of your roving, drawing it out slowly and putting twist in to make an initial length of yarn. ❷Once you have a length of yarn that is long enough to reach from the hook to the shaft

**12** • **Productive Spindling**

below the whorl and back up again, stop, leaving this *leader* on the hook. ❸ Bring the start of the leader to the base of the hook (do not remove it from the hook!), then wind your leader down around the whorl, ❹ around the shaft down, and back up and ❺ through the hook. That initial length of downward-going yarn is your "notch," it is there for you to bring yarn back up against from then on. It acts like a brake, stopping the newer yarn from slipping past.

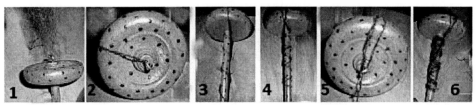

The initial length will be the only downward-going yarn; ❻ from now on, wind on all new lengths as you normally would – take the new yarn out from under the hook, wind it on the shaft, and bring the end back up to the hook. For more about winding on, see "Efficient Wind-On" on page 20.

## Hook

Hook was not just the captain of a pirate ship and Peter Pan's arch nemesis. The hook is a key point of a spindle. Most top-whorl spindles have a hook; bottom-whorl spindles might have a hook or a simple indentation or groove near the top of their shaft. If your spindle has a hook, the hook needs to be sturdy. A soft-metal hook can bend too easily in your carry-all or when the spindle lands hook-first on the floor. The hook should help the yarn center itself.

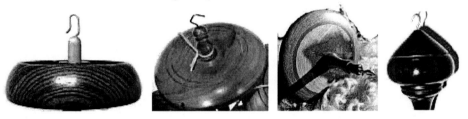

Spindle Hooks: Bosworth Shepherd's Crook, Kundert Diamond, Ledbetter Pigtail (picture by riverpoet), Natalie J

Hooks come in a variety of shapes – shepherd's crook, diamond, pig tail, and an upside down J are typical. The shape of the hook affects where you bring the yarn up to keep it centered. If you view the hook as opening at 12:00 and its base being at 6:00, then for diamond and J hooks, typically bringing the yarn up at 3:00 for clockwise Z spinning or 9:00 for counter-clockwise S spinning centers the yarn. A shepherd's crook is less picky, and may balance bringing the yarn up at 6:00 no matter which direction you spin. The pig-tail tends to center the yarn on its own.

Centering the yarn helps minimize wobble. If your yarn comes from your hand and to the high point of the hook in a line that continues through the center of the spindle's shaft, then when the spindle is twirling, suspended from your yarn, no wobble is being introduced by off-center suspension. This picture shows the yarn coming from hook around the whorl, with the line of the yarn passing down through the center of the shaft.

If the yarn is not in a straight line, gently bend the hook to help the yarn center. Very mild pressure and almost no hook movement may be all that is needed – be careful, as you do not want to permanently damage or loosen the hook when doing this. To protect the smoothness of the hook, use cloth in the teeth of your pliers.

## Shaft Length

The length of the shaft of your spindle affects the weight distribution – a longer shaft is heavier than a shorter one of the same diameter. A very long shaft can add enough weight to make the spindle more likely to gyroscope. If the spindle is rotating in a large circle, with the far end of the shaft tracing a regular circle as the spindle spins, it is *gyroscoping*. Gyroscoping doesn't slow the spindle, but it can be visually distracting.

A one- to two-ounce spindle can balance a ten- to twelve-inch shaft fairly well, only gyroscoping from a very brisk thigh roll and calming down fairly quickly into a straight spin. The thigh roll is the best way to get maximum speed from your spindle.

To thigh roll, right-handers place the spindle shaft between the flat of your right hand and your right thigh. For clockwise twirl, roll the shaft toward your body by dragging your hand over it to make it roll. Left-handers place the spindle shaft between the flat of your left hand and your left thigh, and for a clockwise twirl, roll the shaft away from your body on your left side using the flat of your left hand.

The faster the drag, the more rolling motion, and the faster the spindle spins. To minimize wobble from the thigh roll, keep the spindle vertical – if you are spinning while standing, this means adopting a stork-like pose for the rolling moment to place your thigh horizontal(-ish) to the ground for a good thigh-rolling platform.

Most adult palms are about four inches across, so you will want to keep the bottom four inches of your top-whorl spindle shaft (or the top four inches of your bottom-whorl spindle shaft) cop-free. The rest of the spindle shaft between the end and the whorl is available for cop storage.

Thigh roll top whorl, right hand and leg: toward hip for clockwise Z twist. (left hand on left leg, toward knee)

## Shaft Diameter

If I had a degree in physics, I likely could explain why a smaller diameter shaft gives more momentum for the same effort expended. As it is, I can just tell you – the smaller the shaft, the more speed you will get from the same power of finger-flick or thigh roll. A finger-flick is done by putting the shaft of the spindle between thumb and index finger and setting it rotating with a quick flick of those two fingers. If you are finger-flicking, do this at the thinnest point of your shaft – if the end of your top whorl comes down to a point, grab it at the end; if there's an indent near the top of your bottom whorl, spin it there. Flick the shaft from the side, rather than cupping it from underneath or above, which causes it to wobble.

When choosing a spindle, look for a thinner shaft to get more oomph from your thigh rolls. 3/8" is about the thickest shaft for a reasonably high speed thigh roll; 1/4" will go much quicker, but may warp more easily, especially if it is a long shaft. Half-way between the two, a 5/16" shaft diameter is a good compromise of warp resistance and speed.

Bosworth spindles' shaft Length and diameter vary for each spindle size. The smooth taper lets you slide fiber onto a straw or quill. (photo by turtleknitter)

In addition to diameter, consider overall shaft shape. If it widens at the base, it may have a more balanced spin but you will not be able to slide your cop off onto a storage quill.

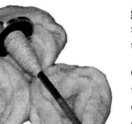

Golding's grooved straight shaft provides excellent grip (photo by arielart)

A tapered spindle shaft allows the cop to slide off easily but it also means if you drop your spindle, the cop may slip off when the spindle hits the ground. Are you past the drop stage of drop spindling? The tapered spindle also gives you a thinner shaft diameter for twirling at the end, a useful feature.

Grooves along the length of the shaft are helpful for providing grip for thigh roll and finger flick twirls, without affecting the ability to slide the cop up or down. Grooves around the circumference should be more carefully considered. Shallow grooves won't hang up the cop, but deeper or decorative curves and turnings may make it difficult to slide a cop off. They can be covered with a tight winding of paper to ease sliding the cop over them.

## Wobble

Bolivian Pushka (large spindle) (photo by ellenspn)

Wobble happens. If you look at the spindles used historically, and even today's tools in Bolivia and beyond, they were made from sticks as grown, possibly carved but nowhere near the perfectly machined and balanced tools made by North American woodturners. Wobble does eat up some of the twirl energy, granted. So we try to avoid it, starting with lathe-balanced spindles. But what do the Bolivians do?

How you twirl your spindle can impart wobble. The key is to keep the spindle vertical. If you finger flick, keep the spindle hanging vertically when you set it rotating. Flick with your palm next to the shaft, not above or below it. If you thigh roll, bring your thigh to horizontal so you can roll your hand with the spindle held vertically. If the spindle wobbles after you start it spinning but otherwise appears balanced, check and check again for any off-vertical approach to spindle twisting. A very high-speed thigh roll can make a spindle gyroscope – that is not a wobble, but is the shaft describing a regular cone. The far tip of the shaft appears to be moving in a circle, as the spindle rotates.

Wobble can be created from the yarn not coming in a straight line from your hand to the hook, and that line pointing down the middle of the spindle shaft. Try placing the yarn through the hook at different places around the whorl to find its most-centered position. If needed, carefully tune the hook, bending it only very gently with small round-nose pliers, to center the yarn.

You may find your spindle wobbling as it fills with yarn. This is due to the cop unbalancing the spindle. With experience, you can wind a more balanced cop, so keep working on this. There will be more about winding on a balanced cop, later.

## Whorl Diameter

Bosworth whorl diameters: Maxi is 3 inches, Midi is 2 ½ inches, and Mini is 2 inches (photo by turtleknitter)

The diameter of the whorl affects the spin-time of the spindle. A wider diameter whorl will typically spin longer than the same shape and weight at a smaller diameter. Also, the wider diameter gives you more room to build a cop before your leader slips because the cop is wider than the whorl.

A whorl diameter of three inches provides a nice storage base in a typical work spindle; smaller whorls down to about 2 inches can also be useful to build cops against. The smaller the whorl diameter, the smaller diameter the shaft should be as well, to ensure the spindle is not too center weighted ~ more about that in a bit.

Spindle Choice • 15

## Whorl Shape

Whorls come in a variety of shapes from a flat disk to a round ball. The flat disk spreads the whorl's weight from rim to center fairly evenly. It tends to give a spindle an even, balanced spin, not super fast or super long. An improvement over the flat disk carves out some of the disk between the rim and the shaft. This changes the mass distribution, improving the effectiveness of the mass at the rim to give longer spin times. Spindle makers go so far as to drill holes all the way through the whorl between rim and shaft, or place very dense materials such as metal on the outer rim, to improve spindle spin times.

*A brass ring and cut-out whorl maximizes the Golding Spindle's momentum (photo by WonderMike)*

A round ball maximizes the weight near the shaft. This shape of spindle can spin quickly, but not for very long. It can be useful for spindling fibers that need a lot of twist to hold together, such as silks, but generally productive spindlers are looking for longer spin time, and will use techniques such as the thigh roll for speed of spin. The round ball shape often appears more squashed and UFO-shaped in turned wood spindles.

Add these two shapes together: a rim-weighted whorl with a thick center whorl gives a long and fast spin. An efficient spindle will have a whorl that has a dished-out ring, leaving wood at the rim and at the center.

Shaft shape also affects the mass distribution – a tapered shaft that is thick near the whorl adds center weight for stability, while also providing a finer diameter for a high-energy flick. Mass near the shaft helps stabilize and prevent gyroscoping or wobble.

*Natalie silk spindle – centerweighted shaft for a fast spin, with a short spin time.*

## Spindle Weight

If you want to pack four ounces of fiber onto your spindle, how important is the weight of the spindle at the start?

The starting weight directly affects the ease of spindling the first half ounce or so of your fiber – when spinning singles, the spring energy of the singles will bring a half- ounce spindle to a halt much faster than it will halt a one-and-a-half-ounce spindle. So it makes sense to start with a spindle that works for you, rather than fighting through the first ounce – 25% of the spindling!

The spindle weight also affects the weight as it fills – a one-ounce spindle adds only one ounce to your four ounces of fiber, giving you five ounces to twirl; while a three ounce spindle makes your work harder near the end, with seven total ounces to twirl at the four-ounce mark.

My own preferences in spindle weights have varied from having one at each gram mark from 3 to 60 grams and scientifically choosing it for the specific weight of fiber, to using whatever looked pretty, showing spindle weight didn't really matter. In the long run, I like to have three spindles on hand to make spindling more enjoyable and efficient:

- A half-ounce or lighter spindle for cobweb spindling – really fine yarns, over 40 wraps per inch. It won't hold much, but at that fine-ness, you get a lot of yardage from just a few grams of fiber. It's light enough to ensure I spin fine at the start, but heavy enough to spin at a reasonable clip.

- A one-ounce spindle for lace, sock, and some DK weight spindling: anything from 30 to 15 wraps per inch, though I will admit to some struggle at the outer ends, thus this is my "mid-weight" spindle with choices above and below for the finer and thicker ends of the spectrum. This also will be the

*Kundert's tapered shaft has nice grip and fine diameter at the end. (photo by stringplayer)*

*Wraps per inch (wpi) is a measure of yarn thickness. Count the number of times your yarn can wrap around a dowel in a one inch space, touching but not crammed together.*

**16 ● Productive Spindling**

plying spindle for the cobweb and lace yarns, as the half-ounce spindle doesn't have the mass to ply two of its cops efficiently.

- A one-and-a-half-ounce to two-ounce spindle for sock to chunky spindling, and plying singles from the one-ounce spindle. For chunky spindling, the one-and-a-half-ounce spindle is a little clunky at the start, but you're producing masses of yarn quickly enough that a more efficient weight is quickly reached.

All of my "dream team" spindles have rim weighting and center weighting in their spindle shape.

You may notice a tendency in the pictures toward Bosworth, Tabachek and Kundert spindles — that is because they are very good spindles, and currently made. Spindle makers come and go — Mongolds were the gold standard in their day; someday Bosworths will be as rare. You may find a first-time spindle maker at a wool festival — evaluate the spindles as tools, not from their lack of fancy turnings or famous name. You may or may not discover the next Bosworth, but regardless you will have a good tool in your hand.

My spindle dream team — Bosworth featherweight in lacewood, Tabachek compact deluxe in zebrawood, and Kundert pinwheel in exotic woods.

## Plying Spindle Choice

For plying, look for a spindle with a wide whorl and rim weighting — the singles want to be plied together, so they will assist with keeping the spindle going. The rim-weighted whorl provides for a longer spin time, and the wider whorl gives more storage space for a larger cop before you exceed the whorl diameter.

When you wind on, you are adding weight at the shaft, thus increasing spin speed, and sacrificing a little bit of spin time. This is why it is helpful to build up your cop like a weaver's pirn, to keep pushing yarn weight out, section by section, before you put more yarn close to the shaft. See "Efficient Wind-on" on page 20 for details.

Your plying spindle can be heavier than your singles spindle for the same yarn weight, since when plying you are working with yarn — the danger of fiber drifting apart is mostly removed.

Left to right: Bosworth mini and plying spindles, Tabachek plying and mini spindles.

Underplied sections may be at risk of drifting apart during plying, so keep an eye on them. If the singles break, it's a weakness in the single, best discovered during spindling rather than while warping your loom or when a lovely shawl is on your knitting needles or crochet hook.

You can fill two small spindles with laceweight, and then ply both together on a larger spindle. I typically choose a one-and-a-half- to two-ounce spindle for most of my plying; generally more toward the light end, as the spindle gains weight fairly quickly from plying, and I can pack more on the spindle before the total weight becomes unmanageable.

| 2-ply yarn weight | WPI | Spindle | Plying Spindle |
|---|---|---|---|
| 0/Lace | 24+ | ½ oz | 1 oz |
| 1/Super Fine, Fingering | 19-22 | ½ - 1oz | 1-1½ oz |
| 2/Fine, Sport | 15-18 | 1 oz | 1½-2 oz |
| 3/Light, DK | 12-14 | 1 - 1½ oz | 1½-2 oz |
| 4/Medium, Worsted | 9-11 | 1½-2 oz | 2 oz |
| 5/Bulky, Chunky | 7-8 | 1½-2 oz | 2 oz |
| 6/Super Bulky | <=6 | 2 oz | 2 oz-plus |

# Productively Filling a Spindle

So you've picked out a spindle or set of spindles that will work for you, and picked up a few techniques on ways to use it productively. Now let's explore getting yarn onto the spindle effectively, starting with the leader, discussing wind-on, and reviewing drafting techniques appropriate for the fiber you are spinning.

## An Efficient Leader

You do not need to spend the time setting up a leader for your spindle – start directly from the fluff you want to spin. If your spindle is a notchless top whorl, see the earlier section on starting from fluff to make yourself a yarn-brake. If your spindle is notched or a bottom whorl, read on.

On handedness – I'm a right-handed person. When I spindle, my left hand holds the fiber supply, and my right hand twirls my spindle and drafts fiber out of my left hand. Lefties can reverse this – hold the fiber in your right hand, and twirl the spindle with your left hand. In this book, I call the hand holding the fiber your *fiber hand* and the hand drafting and twirling the spindle your *spindle hand* or *drafting hand*. Where needed to get the correct direction of spin (on a thigh roll, for example), I'll provide both right- and left-hand specific descriptions.

Start spindling holding your spindle in your spindle hand and putting the hook or shaft tip into the tuft of fiber at the end of your roving (held by your fiber hand), drawing the fiber out thinner slowly and putting twist in by rotating the spindle clockwise with your spindle hand to make an initial length of yarn. For a hookless spindle, your spindle hand will have to do double duty, holding that initial length onto the spindle while twisting it to make the initial length of yarn. Once you have a length of yarn that is long enough to reach from where you want to build your cop on the shaft back up to the hook, plus about a foot, stop. This will be your leader.

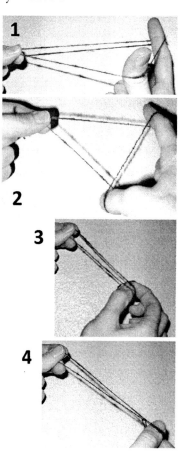

My favorite style of attaching the leader to the shaft is a lark's head knot or snitch knot. This handy knot is formed by ❶ making a triangle with about nine inches of yarn, one hand pinching the very end of the yarn down to the rest of it, and the index finger and thumb of the other hand pointing toward you making the other two corners of the triangle. ❷ Rotate your index finger and thumb, rolling them over the yarn toward the other point so they both have yarn wrapped around them. This looks a bit like the letter 'A'. ❸ Then, touch the ends of index finger and thumb together and nudge the wrap that is on your finger onto your thumb. ❹ You now have a lark's head knot on your thumb – slide this onto your spindle shaft and snug it up. Place it so that when you wind on, the yarn pulls the knot tighter (reverses the direction it comes out of the knot) for maximum effectiveness.

I wind on in the same direction as I spin, so that slippage won't unwind as easily. But if I've forgotten initially, I don't undo and redo – slippage has not been a big issue. So if you prefer to always wind on clockwise, try it and see if it works for you.

Once you've made this knot a few times, it's very quick. It has two additional virtues: it snugs up tight, and it comes undone easily once pulled off the spindle shaft.

Now bring the yarn up to the hook. On a top whorl, bring it through the whorl's notch if you have one, and then up to the hook. Find the most effective location for your leader – behind the hook, to the right of the hook, or to the left. I find for clockwise, or Z, spinning, the right side of most hooks is preferable; while for counter-clockwise, or S, spinning, the left side works better. Try both out, and try behind the hook – see which gives the best result.

You want to have enough leader left over to have four to six inches of yarn left above the hook (or above the bottom-whorl half-hitch – more about that later).

On the bottom whorl, place the lark's head knot just above the whorl and barberpole yarn up the shaft. Then you can twirl the spindle with your fingers, thigh roll, or use Peruvian speed plying.

## Thigh Roll and the Bottom Whorl

Thigh roll with yarn barberpoled up the shaft. Right hand on right leg, rolling toward hip for Z twist. (Left hand on left leg, roll toward knee.)

A bottom-whorl spindle with a reasonably long shaft (ten inches or more) can be thigh rolled. Righties, place the flat of the shaft against your right thigh, with the whorl below your leg, and roll it toward your hip with the flat of your right hand, for clockwise Z twist. Lefties, place it against your left thigh, and roll it toward your knee with the flat of your left hand, for clockwise Z twist.

To be able to do this, you will need to barberpole the yarn up the shaft of the bottom-whorl spindle, so that it does not get in the way. Yes, you will be rolling yarn on your thigh, but the abrasion is minimal so yarn quality is not diminished. Once done winding your cop, spiral yarn around the shaft up to the top, place a half-hitch on the shaft, and perform the thigh roll.

The thigh roll is most useful when spinning singles. When plying, the Andean hand roll is equally effective. But first, let us look at that half-hitch.

## Bottom-Whorl Half-Hitch

One nice feature of bottom-whorl spindles is that there is often no hook to protect. However, this means the yarn is held on by yarn that has to ride up the side of the shaft at the top of the spindle. This means your bottom-whorl spindle is likely to have some wobble inherent in it, since the yarn can't be directly in line with the center of the spindle shaft. Having a thinner shaft near the top helps reduce this, and I've found a good fast twirl from a thigh roll will overcome all but the worst wobble.

On a hookless spindle, a half-hitch is used to hold the yarn on the shaft. This works best if the shaft has an indentation just below the end, to keep the half-hitch from sliding up and off the spindle.

Slipping half-hitch from finger to shaft.

The fast way to make a half-hitch is to hold the spindle in your spindle hand, wind the yarn around your fiber hand's index finger while it is pointing, in line with your spindle, from tip to whorl. Rotate the finger 180 degrees and bring it next to the spindle shaft. That rotation of your finger turned the simple loop into a half-hitch. Now, slip the shaft into the half-hitch on your finger as shown here, and remove your finger. Pull to tighten the half-hitch on the shaft.

The barberpole of yarn up the shaft serves two purposes. One, to enable a thigh roll (or hand roll, when plying); second, to give us some stored yarn for fast half-hitch removal.

When it is time to wind on, pick up the new yarn using the Peruvian butterfly in

**Filling a Spindle ● 19**

your fiber hand so it is kept under mild tension. This is done by wrapping the yarn around two fingers – I use my middle and pinkie fingers – in a figure eight, or butterfly, shape. Wrapping the yarn this way brings the spindle closer so your right hand can reach it, and keeps it under tension so it can be wound onto the spindle easily.

To wind on, ❶hold the lower end of the spindle in your spindle hand and grasp the half-hitch with the thumb and a free finger of your fiber hand. Rotate the spindle with your spindle hand so that the yarn in the barberpole loosens. ❷As soon as the yarn loosens enough, slip a finger from your fiber hand under it and lift the half-hitch off the shaft. Now, wind on your new yarn from the Peruvian butterfly to the cop on your spindle, barberpole up, and place a new half-hitch at the top of the spindle.

Peruvian butterfly: figure-8 wind-up on two fingers of your fiber hand

### Bottom-Whorl Leader

The main challenge I found in bottom-whorl spindling was predicting the length needed for the yarn, to know when to stop winding on. The length is, of course, longer than for a top-whorl spindle. And, it varies with every spindle. So it is useful to check what length you are finding works for you – how much yarn does it take to barberpole up the shaft, make a half-hitch, and still have four to six inches above the hook? Make a mental note of that, and you will find all future estimates much easier than making a new guess each time.

### Efficient Wind-On

Weavers have an advantage when they decide to learn to spin; they have been winding bobbins or pirns for their weaving, giving them a lot of experience in making a clean X wind-on. My preference for the X wind-on is three-fold: it provides more stability on a slick shaft, if your spindle's shaft is highly polished; it stores more yarn per rotation on the spindle shaft than a straight wrapping; and it is less likely to collapse or cut into itself than a straight rotation. It takes some practice to be efficient at making Xs as you wind on, because you need to move the yarn up and down the shaft to make one arm of the X going up, and the other arm coming back down.

To efficiently twirl the spindle while performing the wind-on, turn your top-whorl spindle upside down and twirl the hook on your thigh for speed as you wind; a bottom-whorl spindle can be twirled without turning it upside down. Hold the yarn at about a 45-degree angle spiraling up the shaft a few times, and then, still twirling, hold it at about a 45-degree angle spiraling back down the shaft.

Twirling spindle to wind-on

You will need to manage the yarn as you wind it on, keeping it under mild tension. The Peruvian butterfly is helpful for this. It is a simple wind-on of the new yarn onto two fingers of your fiber hand – ❶with the new length of yarn, pinch the very end between thumb and index finger, and make an infinity symbol, or figure eight, between middle and pinky finger, wrapping two fingers ❷back and ❸forth with a cross-over in the middle. Or, find what works best for you for pinching the end and wrapping – you need not use the same finger arrangement.

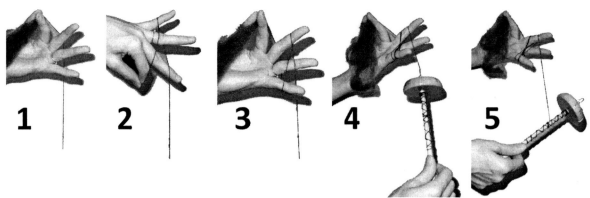

You will find you can walk your fingers up the new yarn (❷,❸) while making this wrapping, ❹until your spindle hand can reach and hold onto the spindle. ❺Then, you can twirl the spindle in your spindle hand as you wind the yarn on, tugging it gently out of the butterfly as needed.

The second part of building an efficient cop is the cop shape. Once you have all the yarn on the spindle, you will want to take it off efficiently to prepare it for plying. There are two useful shapes to build a cop into: a football, or oval shape; and a beehive shape.

Football-shaped cop
(photo by marihana)

The football shape is built by making the X wind-on as long as you want the fiber storage to be on your spindle initially, and gradually moving in from both ends while building the cop outwards. It's a nice wind-on if you plan to slip your cop onto a knitting needle or straw for placement on a lazy kate, or putting your spindle in a spindle kate, for plying or final skeining. One drawback compared to the beehive is that it always adds weight from the shaft, out.

The beehive is built a little at a time. Start by covering about one inch of the shaft with the X wind-on. Make a few layers there, then move out about a quarter inch, winding the initial length and the additional quarter inch together for a few layers. Keep adding quarter inches, building up layers smoothly. Be sure to keep the yarn under medium tension as you wind on, so that the new wrappings on the shaft do not get sloppy or pushed out by the layers above them. The beehive can be slipped onto a needle or straw or used from a spindle kate. It also can be used as an end-feed wind-off of the yarn, a very minimalist-tool way of preparing for plying (see "Plying Technique" on page 34). A nice feature of the beehive is that it builds yarn out at the same time as yarn is added close to the shaft, providing a bit better spindle physics than the football style wind-on.

Beehive cops with X wind-on
(photo by bloomkitty)

Spinning a longer length before winding on is another way to increase efficiency. If you are not yet at arm's reach, but have run out of spin, with a top-whorl spindle and some bottom whorls, you can do a kick start. Hold the spindle vertical between the sides of your feet, even with the balls of your feet, and kick your right foot backward for clockwise (Z) twist or kick your right foot forward for counter-clockwise (S) twist. This can be as effective as a thigh roll, in the right shoes.

If you are left-footed, use a forward left-foot kick for clockwise (Z) twist and a backward left-foot kick for counter-clockwise (S) twist.

**Filling a Spindle** ● 21

You could spin over a balcony for even more length, but consider efficiency – the time it would take to wind up the added length in a Peruvian butterfly (or however) to be able to reach the spindle for winding on, versus the time to unhook or un-half-hitch the leader before winding on. And then there's the long walk you take when the spindle drops ...

## Bottom-Whorl Cop Building

This is done in the same manner as for a top whorl. Again, plan for how you want to wind off.

Kickstart - spindle is between feet; for Z twist, kick back with right foot (as shown here) or kick forward with left foot.

Peruvian spindles have plain wood shafts that are pointed and stick out about two inches below the whorl. They stick their spindles in the dirt to pull off the ends for creating an Andean plying ball.

I doubt, somehow, that you will want to stick your spindle in the dirt – but an end-feed wind-off is a convenient way to take the yarn from the spindle, as the spindle can, and generally will, stay fairly still with a good beehive wind-on. See "Plying Technique" on page 34 for more about the end-feed wind-off.

The cop-winding twirl is easier with a bottom whorl, as you don't need to flip the spindle over, and there is no hook to be delicate with, but instead a sturdier, possibly pointed, bottom of the spindle.

Full bottom whorl (photo by criminyjickets)

## Bottom-Whorl Turkish Spindles

The Turkish spindle is typically a bottom whorl. Turkish spindles have the advantage of presenting you with a wound ball of yarn upon completion – the easiest cop removal, and the cop is ready for easy rewinding into a two-strand ball for plying if you can retrieve the starting point. Luckily, this is simple: tie the starting yarn below the whorl on the shaft – a lark's head knot or whatever kind you prefer; when you pull out the shaft, the starting length should come out with it.

Winding onto the Turkish spindle can be a little less efficient – so decide how you want to wind on, and determine what the minimal movements are for that wind-on. The over-two-arms, under-one-arm wind-on is easy to remember, but to do this you may find yourself making large movements with the spindle or your winding arm, or both.

Turkish with over-2, under-1 wind-on; removed cop, bottom-up, on the left (photo by sockpr0n)

You can also wind on fairly randomly, to build a ball shape. For balance, it's best to make it more regular than random, making Xs that cross over each other on the whorl pieces. Wind one bar of the X a few times, then rotate the yarn around the shaft a quarter turn and wind the other bar of the X a few times.

Turkish spindle X wind-on (photo by Iline)

You may find that an over-two under-one wind-on initially, followed by a more random winding on the built-up surface that maintains a tidy appearance (because "tidy" will be fairly close to "balanced"), may combine the best of both wind-ons.

Clearly this wind-on does not give you a cop that can be pulled off a shaft. However, it does give you a tightly wound one strand ball – with two of them, or just both ends of one, you can wind a two-strand ball easily for plying. Trap the Turkish spindle balls under upturned flower pots or glass measuring bowls and feed the singles out the openings to control them as you wind.

## Efficient Drafting

A way to maximize the effectiveness of your initial twist is to have enough of a starter yarn above the hook to store twist before you start drafting. Six inches, four inches, eight inches – see which maximizes the ability of the spindle to twist while minimally cutting into your draftable length. This length may be affected by how well-prepared your fiber is – fiber that is easy to draft will quickly provide new drafting lengths, while fiber that is more effort to draft will take longer.

Wool locks: Border Leicester (5 in.), Romney, Corriedale, Bond (3 in.) (photo by riverpoet)

When originally learning to spin, we check staple and focus on hand separation – one and a half times the staple length. But as humans we default to a body-driven separation of our hands in front of us, about eight inches apart or so, which is good for most wool, with its four- to six-inch staple length, but a struggle for eight- to ten-inch staple silk or one- to two-inch staple cashmere. If you are finding drafting difficult, check if your hands are far enough apart, or if your fiber is compacted or matted.

As you spindle, consider your hand movements. Is there a way to move them less? The smaller your movements are, the more efficient your spindling is. Your default drafting style may be the most efficient one *for you*. However, if you learn and practice a variety of drafting styles, then you can choose the one that gives you the desired result, without decreasing efficiency.

The two extreme drafting styles to examine are worsted drafting and woolen drafting. Between these is a wide range of semi-worsted-to-semi-woolen drafting.

### Worsted Drafting

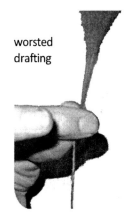

worsted drafting

The shine of a fiber is greatly enhanced with worsted drafting, which promotes smoothness on the surface of the yarn. For this, your spindle (forward) hand is continually pinching the yarn as it controls twist. Twist does not get past the forward hand. Your fiber hand is drafting the fiber while your forward hand is sliding up to let twist into the drafted-out fiber. The drafting triangle between your two hands is always free of twist.

Your fiber hand will move back into the fiber supply to provide more fiber to draft from time to time. When the spindle stops, your fiber hand moves up to the front of the drafting triangle to stop twist from entering the drafting triangle while your forward hand holds the spindle.

**Filling a Spindle • 23**

## Woolen Drafting

Woolen drafting enhances the bounce of the yarn, while not having as smooth an appearance. For this, pinch with your forward hand to prevent twist from moving into the drafting triangle so it is still draftable, but rather than sliding the forward hand, release and quickly re-pinch about half a staple length back from that point once a length has been drafted back with your fiber hand. How far back to re-pinch depends on how long a length you can draft; you may find you only want to re-pinch at an inch, to help maintain a consistent drafting triangle; or you may find you can re-pinch at a full staple length. You can let some twist into the drafting triangle in this method; the only requirement is that you can still draft it down to the thickness you want. If you can't draft the fiber in the triangle, then it has too much twist in it – unroll the twist from it with your forward hand, draft it back, and continue.

woolen drafting

Woolen tends to have a fuzzy surface. Keep finger contact (not pinch) along the length with your forward hand as you move it up to smooth out the surface – this is an appearance change only, the yarn is still woolen spun with woolen's tendency to halo.

## Long-Staple Drafting

The very long staple length of some fibers – silk, Wensleydale, and Suri alpaca in particular – may be more of a challenge. For ease of drafting, your hands should be about one-and-a-half times the staple length apart. Most wools have a four- to six-inch staple, and so naturally our default mode has our hands six to nine inches apart – our hands find that they are effective there, so that is where they gravitate to. With silk, though, its staple length can start at six inches. And a gorgeous Wensleydale wool or Suri alpaca may have an eight- to ten-inch staple. So your hands will be fighting a tug-of-war, each holding onto an end of the same fibers, rather than helping one another draft and create yarn.

There are two things to try. First, consciously examine the staples of the fibers. Then place your hands one-and-a-half times that far apart. An eight-inch staple means your hands need to be twelve inches apart – a whole foot! You may find you start out at a foot, but your hands creep back to their default. Try something visual as a reminder – perhaps place a big picture book in your lap that is a foot long, a child's ruler, or use a spinner's lap cloth or piece of gingham fabric with one-inch squares.

Second, consider spinning these super-long fibers from the fold. Tug off a piece of roving or top from the end so it is about the length of the staple of the fiber, and fold it in half over your fiber-hand's index finger. Draft from the tip of that finger. You've effectively cut the staple length in half, back down to where your body's default hand placement works fine. When there's just a little left at that half-staple-length, break off a new piece, put it over your finger, and join onto the remaining length to continue.

drafting from the fold

Staple-length of fiber folded over index finger

Draft from the top (middle) of the folded fiber

## Short-Staple Drafting

Finally, for extremely short staple lengths, there is another method to consider. Cotton, cashmere, yak, and camel have extremely short staple lengths; these fibers benefit from point of twist drafting.

In point of twist drafting, twist is entering the drafting triangle just as you are drawing back on it. Keeping this point consistent gives a consistent amount of twist and a consistent thickness of yarn. This is a balance point that you spend some time searching for – how fast to spin your spindle, how fast to draft the fiber. Also, once you have a length spun, you will pinch off in front of the drafting triangle, add twist until you have a strong, good-looking two-ply, and then wind it on your spindle.

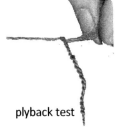

plyback test

Check the two-ply with a plyback test: fold four inches of newly spun yarn on itself to create a two-inch plied length between your fiber hand and the spindle. For these super-fine fibers, the plyback test should have no open O at the bottom, ever. I've found that when I've strayed from that tenet, my singles separate during plying. Then my mouth is open in an O!

Once the new length is wound on, you will want to start the draft a bit before you release the twist to travel back – this is because you added extra twist to the yarn wound onto the spindle; that twist is in the leader too, and will come roaring back to your drafting triangle. Prepare for this by unrolling the drafting triangle slightly to make it twist-free, pinching in front of it, then holding twist out of it as you first start your spindle twirling.

Having a lightweight spindle can make all the difference with these super-fine fibers. A half-ounce spindle is very effective for spinning cashmere, cotton, and angora into lovely laceweight yarns. Its weight won't present too much of a challenge to the fiber, while with rim and shaft whorl shaping, it will provide the momentum needed for a long and fast spin.

## How Full Can You Fill A Spindle?

You can put as much fiber on a spindle as you like. With practice, your cop will be more balanced, so wobble will not be a major factor as your spindle fills. So the key is to determine what is comfortable with you, and how to deal with the curve balls a full spindle can throw at you. If you've dealt with all the curve balls, and it isn't comfortable, then it's full!

Full Ethan Jacob: 1.1oz/31g fiber on a 0.2oz/6g spindle (photo by marihana)

Consider how much fiber you will be spindling, and how many spindles you want to fill; perhaps you have four ounces, and want to fill two spindles to ply from – then you need only put two ounces on each spindle; that's easily done on a production spindle. Or, you are spinning laceweight yarn: you might put a half ounce each on two spindles, ply that, and repeat until you are done. Perhaps you have a pound of wool and want to see just how much you can get on your spindle – go for it!

A featherweight spindle tends to be able to hold about one-third to one-half its weight in fiber before becoming uncomfortable to spin. The featherweight is used to spin laceweight yarn – a tricky task that requires a light spindle; weight is the key to success with the finest yarns. Some spindlers master spinning lace on heavier spindles, and can pack more onto their featherweights. See "Drafting Singles on Full Spindles" on page 27 for some advice on managing the additional weight.

A sturdy production spindle – a one- to two-ounce spindle – can easily manage three times its own weight in fiber or more. Two issues tend to come up as the spindle fills: the leader slips, and the spindle-plus-yarn weight begins to affect drafting, pulling the fiber apart before you have enough twist in to make it yarn.

My 1.8-ounce (51g) notchless top-whorl spindle began slipping once it was holding one ounce of fiber. So I wound the yarn around just below the hook, undoing it at the start of each wind-on and redoing it at the end.

You can keep building up the cop down the shaft and in diameter. As you build down, be sure to leave room to twirl – palm width to two inches, minimum. As you build out, it can build up even wider than the whorl. Be sure to consider how you will wind off, as if you build layers in a football shape, you won't be able to do an end wind-off, but will need to slide the cop onto a quill for a lazy kate or put the spindle on a kate or in a large bowl, to feed the yarn off from the side.

That is only stage one of slipping. Stage two comes a bit later. Once it starts slipping with the under-whorl end wind-on, you will need to change to a more secure wind-on. Now, wind ending at the bottom of the shaft, then go once around the shaft directly, and *straight up* (no winding) to the whorl and the hook. The yarn bracing against the cop, coupled with the tight wind on the shaft, prevents slippage. This wind-on takes practice, to determine what length of yarn you need at the end to fit around the shaft, up the cop, and still have about six inches above the hook. You will need to undo the shaft-lock each time before winding on the new length, or your shaft will quickly fill with these.

These are my two preferred methods, though I've seen others used successfully as well. You can wind around the hook two times – this works for a while, but as the weight of the spindle grows, this will slip too. You can put a half-hitch on the hook itself. This lasts for a while longer than the double wrap, but can be a little more work to do and undo, even with the speed half-hitch, because the hook is so thin in diameter.

## Rate of Spindling

What is efficient spindling? For me, it was spindling about an ounce of roving to about a 15 wpi single (so it will work up into a worsted weight two-ply) in about one-and-a-half hours. I was not racing, merely spindling while the after-dinner evening routine of my house unfolded around me. The cop on that spindle stayed relatively balanced even with four ounces of fiber!

Fiber preparation is one of the biggest impacts on the rate of yarn production when spindling. If you have roving or fiber full of vegetable matter (VM – hay, seeds, weeds), you will be spending much of your spindling time picking out the VM. If you have well-processed roving or top or well-organized locks, your time will be more focused on twirling, drafting and winding on.

Wound just below whorl and then up to hook

Wound around shaft below cop and then taken up side of cop to whorl and hook.

Wound twice around hook

The good and the awful: left, lovely space-dyed top; right, sliver full of bits of hay and seeds. Lessons learned: nothing beats seeing fiber in real life to be sure it's VM-free.

The wind-on is usually the second sticking point for people after the quality of fiber; twirling the spindle to wind on helps, as mentioned earlier. Turn your top-whorl spindle over and twirl its hook on your thigh to speed winding on, or twirl your bottom whorl on your thigh directly.

Bosworth with lovely X wind-on (photo by lline)

## Balanced Cop

Which brings me to this ... cops tend to get unbalanced. An unbalanced cop makes the spindle wobble, making your twirl less efficient. Building a more balanced cop takes practice. Practice making a good-looking wind-on under moderate tension. I say good-looking, because a balanced wind-on is just that — appealing to the eye. I've seen some wind-ons taken to extremes, looking like the God's Eye weavings from summer camp in my formative years. They are gorgeous, and I noticed the spindles they are on are *very* full.

## Drafting Singles on Full Spindles

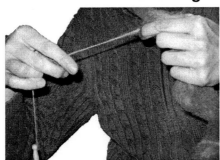

Singles get harder to spin as the spindle gets heavier — the pull really accelerates drafting. You can minimize this by drafting horizontally while the spindle hangs vertically, as shown here. Don't let more than the staple length of fiber hang unspun, and keep a firm pinch at the start of the drafting triangle. Control the twist moving into the drafted section by sliding your hand across the drafted yarn (worsted style) or short pinch-jumps, less than the staple-length (woolen style). Draft horizontally with your drafting hand to provide more fiber for twist to move into.

## Finding More Time to Spindle

I've been known to spindle while the tea is brewing

Spindling is a small-space activity that can be crammed into spare moments; spindling while walking is a great way to add value to your walk, and deserves its own discussion, later. Another solution is to have your spindle with you at your time sinks — the places that bog you down for a few minutes at a time.

Is it watching something under the broiler? That's five or ten good spindling minutes. Is it waiting for the kettle to boil, after the teapot is ready? Another four minutes.

There's also the doctors and dentists offices, the post office line, the bank, watching TV, any time when you're waiting for someone else.

Consider using the speaker feature on your phone, or getting a phone headset for the office — plenty of spindling time waiting to be utilized. I was surprised how much spindling I got done, just having a spindle project near my computer — rather than get frustrated during boot-up or a big file downloads, I'd spin a length or two of yarn. I was relaxed and ready to focus on the computer once it was ready for me again.

Spindling kept handy during downloads and podcasts (photo by breyerchic04)

Keep (or take) a project in your car — that way when you are waiting for an appointment, or your child's concert to start, you can fill the time with spindling. Better yet, if there's another driver, let them drive and spindle as passenger. It may be a non-optimal environment, but it's otherwise free time. I plied 2.4 ounces of two-ply sock yarn as a passenger in a car over a week's vacation. It seemed slow at the time because there was room for just two feet before winding on. But, it let me perfect the twist, unwind for consistency, *and it got done.* You choose — maybe knitting's better for passenger time. Just have an option, so you can use down time for your pursuits.

Spindle projects tucked here and there are great ways to fill otherwise idle moments. Be sure to keep your spindle and fiber safe — a stiff box or container so nothing can crush it or soak it. Use the fiber as padding around the spindle, and consider protecting the hook. The clear vinyl tubing in the plumbing section of your hardware store comes in a variety of diameters — take your biggest shaft-top hooked spindle, and buy a short length of tubing to make several hook protectors for your spindles.

wooden carrier and silk-lined pouch

hooks protected with vinyl tubing

For a portable project, look for a container with a handle or straps for easy carrying, and stiff sides (cardboard, plastic, wood) for protection. Keep it fully portable — use your arm as a niddy-noddy, or put the tools in the container that you most like to use.

## Putting the Spindle Down

At some point, you will need to put the spindle down. How can the yarn be stored so as not to lose twist? Should you break off the unspun roving, or not? Consider where you will be putting the spindle. If you are putting it on a table or shelf, you might leave the roving attached to get back to it; if you are packing it up in a carry-all, will the roving get tugged in and out as you pack and unpack the spindle, possibly breaking in a less controlled manner? If so, you might be better off breaking off the unspun roving — to do this, draft out a little bit so you have a nice staple length ready to join onto when you start again.

The roving has been broken off; the end is wrapped around the spindle shaft.

The last length of spun yarn can be wrapped around the shaft below the cop (above the cop, on a bottom-whorl spindle) a few times, and the roving on top of it as a "wool velcro" to hold it together. Or, you can wrap the end of the yarn around the hook a few times to hold it stable. This will keep the twist in the singles, or will tidily hold your plying until you are ready to continue.

Since the final bit of yarn and fuzz is wound on a bare part of the shaft, the end is easily located for restarting. If you put your fingers on top of that wind-on and rotate to loosen it, it will easily lift off the final bit of fuzz, ready to join and continue.

End of yarn plied back on itself, then wrapped around shaft between spinning sessions.

For singles, if your fiber is more slippery and won't stick onto the shaft or hook easily, take the last six inches of new yarn and let it ply back on itself. This end will then be stable and hold the twist in; wrap it around the cop or even use it to hold onto the shaft with a half-hitch so the singles will stay in place and hold the twist.

When you are ready to start again, unroll the last length of yarn, unply it from itself, join on a new fiber supply, and begin.

## Managing Fiber

You might think that keeping all your fiber in one continuous length would be the most efficient for spindling. However, then you have to manage that length — winding it carefully onto a distaff so it comes off smoothly; or draping it like a boa on clothes that it can slide easily over without slipping off unexpectedly. Eventually, no matter what, you will have to add on a piece of fiber due to an unexpected break in the fiber supply.

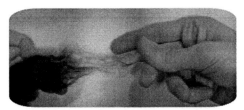

Staple length overlay of new and old fiber for a textbook join

Getting efficient at joins will provide you with a quick continuation of your spindling. For a good join, overlay old and new at greater than staple length, with no (NO, *NO)* twist anywhere. Draft them together and continue. For more join methods see "Join Techniques", page 30.

Once you are good at joins, consider the advantages of short lengths of fiber:

- The fiber won't matt in your hand.

- It is more comfortable to use a short length of fiber on a hot day: even cool silk does not react well to a warm hand.

- There is no preparation time for the fiber – tear off a foot or so, and spin. You can keep the supply handy in a tote or basket.

- If you are spinning a blend, spinning short lengths will ensure you do not get too unbalanced in your yarn – all of the fiber in your hand will be spun into yarn before the next piece is joined on, so if the silk is the last to be spun in, it will show up regularly rather than all at once, at the end of a longer piece.

## Consistency of Spinning

Efficient spinning is also consistent – this gives the most regular result, is easy to ply consistently, and easy to work with as yarn in your knitting, crochet, weaving, embroidery, nalbinding, …. Sometimes we strive for thick-and-thin, or variable twist, or other novel features, but those yarns are spun for a particular result rather than for speed and efficiency.

Spindle-spun worsted weight singles

Consistent singles can be aided by balancing out the twist between lengths of newly spun yarn. To do this, use the Peruvian butterfly to wind up half of the yarn between your fiber hand and the spindle; unwind some yarn from the spindle's cop – the twist will move between the old-spun and new-spun to evenly spread. Then, wind all the yarn onto the cop.

For consistency in your singles, with every spin of your spindle, start with the same leader length above the hook and strive for the same strength of twirl and the same length and thickness of draft.

If the thickness of your singles varies, be aware that twist travels to thin spots – if a thick spot is greater than staple length, it can drift apart – especially when plying! Also, because twist will gravitate to the thin spots, a very thin spot can be over-twisted enough to snap the fibers.

You can't fix your singles twist or thickness issues during plying – only when they are singles. To fix twist, you must add or remove twist as needed. To fix a thick spot, untwist a staple length's worth of singles with the thick spot in the middle. With that length untwisted, you can then draft the thick spot out. Remove your fingers, and the twist moves back in. There's a longer length here now, so add a little more twist to match the rest of the yarn.

Thin spots don't have as simple a solution – the only way to fix them, is to break off the yarn before the thin spot, remove the length with the thin spot in it, unfluff the new end of the yarn for at least a staple length, join on and continue.

As your spindle fills, it gets heavier. There will be greater pull as the spindle weight increases. This affects two things: it takes more effort to get the same speed of twirl, and the greater pull will cause the fiber to draft more – so you need more twist if you are drafting more, but it is harder to get since it takes more effort. Being aware of this puts you half way to compensating for it.

Use a plyback test regularly on your yarn to ensure it has the same twist each time. The plyback test is done by folding a four-inch length of singles on itself to see if you like the appearance of the balanced two-ply. Once you have a two-ply that you like, keep a sample of this spun yarn to compare to. Break off a one-foot length, wrap it around a business card, fuzz out one end and fold the other end on itself in a two-ply. The fuzzed out end shows how much fiber was in the drafting triangle; the single shows how thick your single should be; and the two-ply shows how much twist to put into the singles.

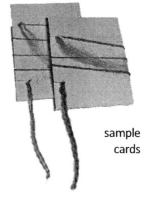

sample cards

When you first start filling a spindle, do the plyback test more frequently until you see a consistent result, and then do it less frequently as you develop consistency.

Let's talk about twist angle for just a second ...

- 17 degrees is soft twist

- 25 degrees is knitting twist

- 35 degrees is weaving or sock twist (hard wearing)

Consider the use of your yarn in choosing a twist angle. Will the yarn be rubbed heavily in the making, like a warp on a loom; or will the final item be roughly used, like the socks inside your boots? Then a high twist angle is recommended. Will the yarn be heavily fulled, or used in a decorative item? Then lower twist is appropriate.

Protractor used to measure twist angle on this yarn ... it has about a 30-degree angle of twist.

Some singles twist is removed when plying; in a balanced twist, the final twist in the singles is balanced by the twist in the ply. The experts disagree on how much twist is removed; so instead measure: if your washed skein hangs open without twisting on itself, it is balanced.

Your sample on the card is balanced; when plying, you may choose to under-ply or over-ply, instead. Under-plied yarn is good for lace knitting – the stitches open up and lie flat. Over-plied yarn is good for work garments, socks and gloves, as it has a strong surface that resists wear. A balanced yarn gives maximum bounce, leaving the fiber in the singles parallel along the length of the yarn.

Above: high-twist wool 2-ply
Below: low-twist silk 2-ply
spindlespun by sherie
(photos by sherie)

## Join Techniques

My *textbook join* is this: have a staple length or more of fiber remaining completely unspun, drafted out fairly fine but not quite as fine as you are spinning. Draft out the beginning of the new length of fiber you're

joining on similarly. Lay these two drafted-out sections on top of each other. The new fiber should start a little bit after the twist stops in the old fiber/yarn. Now, before adding twist, co-draft these two pieces together, down to the thickness you plan to spin. They should meld into one fiber and make an invisible, strong join. (See picture in "Managing Fiber", page 28.)

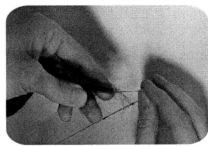

Worsted join: hold yarn on fluffed out roving, add twist until it grabs onto the fiber, then draft back to form the join.

This works great with grabby fibers. With slippery fibers, I have about a 75% success rate. So, I've adopted two other joins: one is a worsted join, for spinning worsted. For this, you fan out the end of the new fiber, and hold the fanned out ends at about a 45-degree angle to the spun yarn, an inch or so above the unspun end. Really! Fiber next to yarn! As you add twist to the yarn, it will grab onto the fanned out end and make a join for you. Once the yarn has grabbed onto the fiber, draft the new fiber supply away from the yarn, and then draft as before.

V-join: New fiber on the left, "V" of fiber at the end of the yarn on the right.

The second is a *V-join*, introduced to me by Kaye Collins at the Whidbey Island Spin-In. Her work with alpaca fiber is a terrific in-depth study of woolen and worsted and its impact on a particular fiber. For the V-join, you fan out the remaining staple-length of completely unspun fiber at the end of your spun yarn, and draft out a staple-length point in your new fiber supply. Sandwich the point inside the V and draft them together. Start adding twist once it is as thick as needed for your yarn. This join is very smooth in appearance and strong, as long as you have the staple length amount and you draft them together before adding twist.

If you don't have a staple length of unspun fiber, undo twist. If your yarn broke at a thin spot, re-break it further up at a thick spot so you can have a staple length of unspun fiber. Having that length completely unspun is the key to success with the textbook join and Kaye's V-join.

## Maximize Productivity

If your focus is to maximize yarn production, then start with well-prepared fiber that is all the same staple length, for the fastest drafting. A blend of fibers or a roving may contain different staple lengths, so test the fiber first. A commercial top will be all the same staple length, but it may be fairly compacted.

spindle and batts (photo by leesy)

You may find it easier to draft open uncompacted fiber or to draft slightly compacted fiber — try your fiber as it comes, then try opening it up or compacting it to see which works easiest for you. Compacted but not matted fiber can be opened up by breaking off a foot-long length of roving or top, or strip a wrist-sized piece along the length of a batt, and then snapping the piece like a whip; predrafting is more effective, but slower. Take an uncompacted fiber and roll it between your hands to compact it, then see how well it drafts in that form.

With consistent staple length, the draft is consistent; you don't end up drafting all long fibers, leaving shorter fibers behind, or having to work them in as you go, taking more effort in drafting.

Staple length in your normal range will be most efficient. Most people spin wool fibers with three- to five-inch staple length. Silk and longwools put your hands further apart than normal, unless they are your usual fibers.

**Filling a Spindle • 31**

Merino and cashmere can be very short – they draft apart very easily with a heavy spindle pulling on them. Your hands have to be closer than normal, which means more clipped, shorter movements to control the drafting pull of the spindle as well.

Fiber diameter drives default yarn thickness. If you spin a fine fiber, it is easiest to spin a fine yarn – spinning thick merino singles is more difficult and slower than spinning thin merino singles.

Anne Fields found that you can maximize a yarn's hand if handspun two-ply from it has twists per inch equal to the crimps per inch, and wraps per inch equal to twice the crimps per inch. This gives the wool's natural curl a chance to maximize its effectiveness.

Interestingly, finer fibers tend to have more crimps per inch – so you will generally find spinning to the crimp a natural result.

For efficiently spinning fine yarn, start with a fine fiber such as merino; for efficiently spinning a medium weight yarn, start with a medium fiber such as Romney.

Fighting how thickly a fiber wants to be spun will slow you down, unless you get a lot of practice at it – so if it is your desire to spin laceweight Wensleydale, invest the time in making it a natural task for your hands.

## Spin Direction

So far I've been directing you to spin the standard directions – clockwise singles for Z twist and counter-clockwise plying for S twist. These are called Z twist and S twist because the bar in the middle of each letter matches the angle of twist in the yarn.

These are standard directions of twist in the knitting community, because English style knitting usually benefits from these directions being used. Crocheters and Continental knitters may benefit from reversing the single and plying twist directions– they will tend to open up and split Z-single/S-ply yarns. Weavers are much more diverse, sometimes using Z/S warps and S/Z wefts to use the conflicting twist angles for interesting surface light effects.

Something to consider is how many plies you want – singles are fastest to spin, as once spun, they are done. They remain active twist, which affects your fabric. Two-plies come next, as you spin two strands, ply, and are done. Plied yarns add strength and can be balanced or have more controlled twist in them, for more regular behavior in your fabric. A three-ply takes longer, as you have one more ply to spin. Three-ply yarns are rounder and knit into a denser, more insulating fabric.

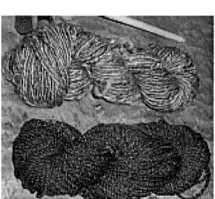

Top: singles; Bottom: cabled yarn. Both worsted weight spindle-spun

Cabled yarns are very straightforward on a spindle, and create a very strong surface due to their nature. They are made by reverse-plying (Z direction) two very overplied standard two-plies. First, spin your singles Z normally; then spin a two-ply S with extra twist so it is overplied; finally, cable-ply two of your two-plies Z to make a balanced, cabled yarn. A cable yarn is created when the final surface looks like a string of pearls or grains of rice.

This cable yarn has a final Z direction – if you desire a final S direction, then start with S-spun (counter-clockwise) singles, ply Z, and cable-ply S.

**32** ● **Productive Spindling**

Guanaco laceweight 2-ply spindle-spun by ellenspn (photo by ellenspn)

Lizzy Kate for plying (photo by bloomkitty)

Crepe yarn spindle-spun by lline: a 2-ply reverse-plied with an S-twist yarn, this is a close relative of cabled yarn (photo by lline)

# Productive Plying

## Plying Technique

The Andean plying popular among U.S. spinners is actually a trick used to use up all the singles of two uneven balls. True Andean plying is a very fast technique for spindle plying. The key to efficiency is to prewind a two-strand ball, or three-strand for three-ply. It is important to maintain even tension on the strands as the ball is wound — the whole time! — to prevent snarls and pigtails.

When one ball ends and the other has some remaining, the spindler would wind the rest of it up into an Andean plying bracelet, splice the end of the shorter ball with the final end of the long ball by overlaying them, and then continue winding the rest of the yarn from the Andean plying bracelet. This is a two-ply technique, clearly.

See "Andean Plying Bracelet" on page 36 for instructions.

Andean plying ball — 2 strands wound in courses - same path several times, then a new path - under even tension

The ball would be wound either directly from two spindles-full, or each spindleful might be wound into a ball first and then the plying ball wound from them. With a beehive build-up, you can often tilt your spindles up and feed off the ends, unwinding the cops without rolling the spindles. Putting your spindle on a flat tray with sides will keep it from rolling away while you wind off it, if the yarn causes it to roll around.

Another ply solution: wind singles onto cardboard tubes, and place the tubes on a knitting-needle kate (photo by artsyfish)

Or, you may want to slide the cop off your spindle onto straws to put on a lazy kate. If you have a shoebox and knitting needles, you can make your own kate, by pushing the needles through across the short side of the box. Use needles small enough for the straws, or push the cops directly from spindle to knitting needle. There are also spindle kates for holding spindles of singles for plying.

Winding the ball need not be scientific. ❶Start with several (say, five to ten) winds around two fingers. ❷Take that off your fingers and wind a few times around its middle. ❸Fold it in half and wind around that a few times; this is your core. ❹Now, wind around it, rotating the ball a bit after every few winds (each group is a *course*) to create a sphere of wound yarn. Remember to keep even tension on both strands so they lie next to each other throughout the winding.

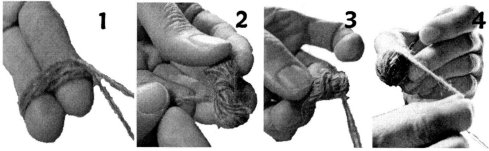

When doing this the first few times, you may find it easier to start with a small ball of felt or paper in the core. It gives you something to hold onto from the start.

**34** • **Productive Spindling**

With this two-strand ball, you are ready to ply. You can do this just like spinning singles, with a thigh roll or finger flick.

First, you need to make a leader. Since these are already spun yarns, let a foot or so of the two-strand ball ply itself as it wants; if your singles are stale, it may be underplied, but for our purposes that will work. Use this length to make a lark's head knot (see "An Efficient Leader" on page 18) or slip-knot to hold the yarn on the shaft. With this as your self-leader, you are ready to begin just as you did for singles, except that your plying will be done in the opposite direction.

The two-strand ball can be held in your hand, pinned onto your shirt (if wound in courses), put under an upside down flower pot (feed through the drain hole), or put under an upturned glass measuring container (feed through the opening at the spout).

This leader does mean you don't have a yarn brake on a notchless spindle — the techniques used on spindles as they fill can be used earlier, as needed, when plying on a notchless spindle.

Since you are handling yarn already, you need not worry about fiber drifting apart. This gives you additional options for twirling your spindle.

With a top-whorl spindle, you can unroll a length until the spindle reaches your feet. Then, holding the spindle vertical between the sides at the balls of your feet, kick your right foot forward for counter-clockwise (S) twist or kick your right foot backward for clockwise (Z) twist.

Left-footed? Kick your left foot backward for counter-clockwise (S) twist or kick your left foot forward for clockwise (Z) twist.

The plying direction is typically *opposite* the singles direction. If you are unsure which way to ply, suspend the spindle from a length and see which way it starts going on its own. That is the direction to ply.

With a bottom-whorl spindle, unroll a length of about two feet or 2/3 of a meter from your two-strand ball; hold the ball in your left hand or pin it to your shirt. You'll need to keep part of your palm free, because you will start the spindle twirling with a Peruvian hand roll. ❶To do this, hold the top of the shaft against the palm of your left hand with the flat of the fingers of your right hand. Now, briskly roll the spindle by rolling it with the flats of your fingers (similar to the thigh roll motion). ❷Roll it away from you for counter-clockwise (S) twist (shown here) or move your right hand toward you for clockwise (Z) twist. ❸As you set the spindle rolling with the Peruvian hand roll, it will fly in an arc until it reaches the length of the loose yarn, and twist will quickly travel into that length. With practice, this becomes a terrific way to impart twist quickly.

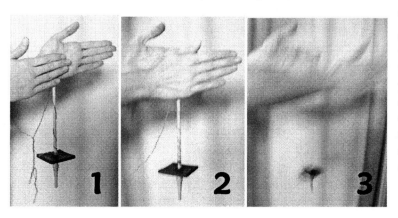

Top or bottom whorl, draft more out from the ball once the initial length has twist. Use the Peruvian butterfly to reach your spindle; use the same cop-building as with singles, considering how you want to remove the fiber when you are done — perhaps even putting it directly on a quill for weaving.

Productive Plying ● 35

## Andean Plying Bracelet

This bracelet is used to make a winding that you can pull from both ends, to finish off the larger of your two spindlefuls into your two-strand plying ball. It is best described in picture steps.

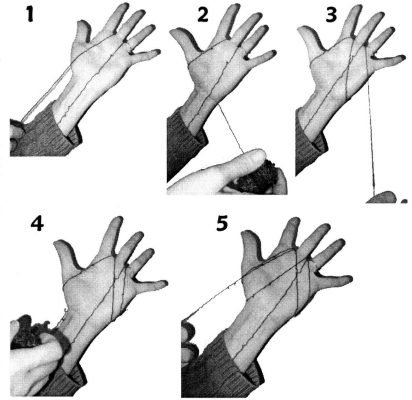

❶ The 2-strand ball is stuffed down my sleeve, and the remaining ball of the first spindleful is in my hand. I wrap it around my middle finger from left to right and bring it over to the thumb side of my hand.

❷ I wrap the yarn behind my hand, from thumb-side to pinky-side.

❸ From the pinky side, I come up around my middle finger and back down to the pinky side.

❹ I wrap the yarn behind my hand from pinky-side to thumb-side this time.

❺ Now I wrap the yarn around my middle finger, meeting up with the first strand at my middle finger and following its path once I do meet up with it.

Repeat steps ❷ to ❺ until all of the yarn has been wrapped around your hand this way. Don't wrap too tightly, or your middle finger will be pulled forward.

Once you have the bracelet wound, slip out your middle finger, move the bracelet to your wrist, and overlap the very end with the single that ended early. Keep winding your two-strand ball, pulling the two strands out from the Andean plying bracelet as you wind.

## Beauty-wave Plying Bracelet

If there is not too much left, and there may not be, you may find it easier to wind around the outside of the four fingers of your fiber hand while it holds the initial two-strand plying ball.

Start with the two-strand ball held under the thumb of your fiber hand. Holding the remains of the larger spindleful (on the spindle, a single strand ball, or on a storage quill) in your spindle hand, wind it around your fiber hand's fingers and the 2-strand ball. Don't trap the ball there, keep it able to pop out toward the end of your fingers.

Once you have all the yarn wound, take the two-strand ball out and hold it in your spindle hand. Remove a finger (I start with my pinky) from the wrapping strands to give them a bit more wiggle room, or slide it down to your wrist if it's loose enough. Take the outer end yarn and overlay the end of the yarn on the two-strand ball by an inch or two.

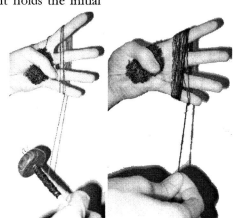

Winding the beauty-wave plying bracelet

**36 ● Productive Spindling**

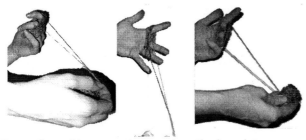

Fingers "wave" between the strands as the bracelet unwraps

Now that you have two strands again, and can continue winding the ball. You will find you can bring the inner strand out of the wrap at the same rate as the outer strand by waving your fingers back and forth as you gently tug on the ends.

Patsy Zawistoski named this method "beauty-wave plying". She teaches this method for plying samples on the spinning wheel in videos and workshops.

## Consistency in Plying

Avoid having to re-ply by being consistent throughout.

Keep a ply sample to visually match each length against; this can be a simple mental image, or a physical sample showing what you are aiming for, to lay your newly spun next to for a physical comparison.

Singles, once they have sat even five minutes, begin to set their twist. The warm bath of the finished skein re-energizes their twist, so you will need to ply to match their original twist to get the effect you want. Taking a short sample of freshly spun singles, plying it to your desired amount (underplied, balanced, or overplied), and wrapping it around a card gives you a physical sample for comparison.

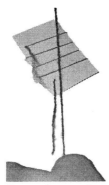

Comparing yarn to sample card

If you have no fresh singles to sample-ply, take your stale singles, break off and fold an eight-inch length on itself, knot the ends in place, and place it in a sink of warm water. The twist will reactivate and the sample will ply as newly spun singles. Squeeze out the water and use this as your balanced-ply sample.

Because your singles are likely to be at least a little bit stale, they will not be able to tell you when their twist is balanced – when their twist is balanced, they will kink up as if they are overplied. You can use this to your advantage – match your sample, and then see how much the newly plied length wants to twist on itself (a ply-back test of your plied yarn). From then on, repeat this "stale yarn" plyback test on your plied yarn to see if you are getting the same amount of "extra" twist. That extra twist will disappear when the skein is washed in warm water to be finished.

Another way to examine plied yarn for balance is to examine the direction of the fibers in the singles. The fibers in a balanced plied yarn (no matter how many plies) lie parallel along the length of the fiber. An underplied yarn's fiber in the singles will still tilt in the same direction as the original spinning (Z if clockwise, S if counter-clockwise). An overplied yarn's fiber in the singles will tilt in the direction of the ply.

To see the fibers in the yarn, use a strong light or daylight and sharp eyes. You can do this test once, and then use the "stale yarn" ply-back test described earlier.

Now, balance in the plying need not be perfect. A slight amount of overplying or underplying in the yarn will not affect the knit stitch or warp the woven fabric. Your skein may still hang open when washed, even without rough finishing of the yarn. And even a strongly underplied or overplied skein will behave like balanced yarn if given a rough finish. The extra twist in the surface will add durability, as will the slight fulling in the finish. See "A Full Spindle!" on page 40 for information on rough-finishing yarn.

An underplied yarn is useful for lace knitting, as the stitches will lie flat and open up to display the lace to best effect.

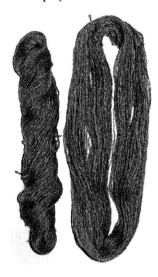

It's all in the finish: the same two skeins of spindle-spun Shetland 2-ply.

On the left, before washing: the skein on the far left looks overplied, its neighbor looks balanced.

On the right, after washing: you can see that the left skein is balanced and that the skein on the far right is actually underplied.

An overplied yarn provides a strong surface for durability, useful in socks and work gloves.

In plying, you can also use several of the consistency methods used for singles:

- Unwind some of the last plied before winding on the new length, to let twist even out between the old and new lengths.

- Use the same strength of twirl, length of leader above the hook, and final length plied for each new length plied.

The concrete measures of plied yarn are twists per inch and twist angle. Twist angle is consistent across yarn thicknesses in terms of showing durability. Twists per inch may be easier to measure to maintain consistency between lengths, however, so it may also be used. A thinner yarn will have more twists per inch at the same twist angle as a thicker yarn.

## Broken Singles When Plying

There may be a time when your singles break when plying. This could be from a section of underspun singles drifting apart, or from a very thin spot breaking. Take a note of why it broke so you can work on improving that aspect of your singles.

To continue, ❶lay the two broken ends over each other and continue. If you are working from a two-strand ball, there may not be much length for an overlap – but with practice, you won't be breaking the singles during plying. Should a break happen with feltable fiber, you might want to do a spit-splice or felted join at that point in the plying, to lightly felt the break together for strength and allow you to continue plying from there. To do that, ❷wet the two ends and the other single, line them all up for plying, and ❸roll them between your two palms until you've generated a bit of heat. ❹They should be lightly felted, if not continue rubbing and re-check until they are.

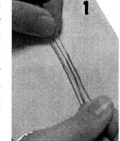
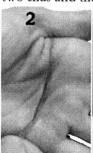

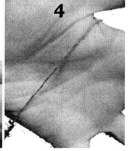

1  2  3  4

If a single breaks while winding the plying ball, overlay it for one to two inches and continue winding.

## Yarn Improvements

If you plan to full or rough finish your skein, wait a moment before doing that. Let it have its first soak without agitation, squeeze out the water, and take a look at the skein. Look it over. Is the ply twist consistent? Put the skein on your wrists or a squirrel cage skeiner, and snap it to help the twist move where it wants. Rotate the skein a bit and repeat this for each length to help twist move around a little as it wants to find balance. This can fix small imbalances, and also gives you a chance to look for any long runs of over– or under– plied yarn.

Those lengths can only be fixed by directly respinning those sections… this is fast on a wheel, but not so fast on a spindle, as you have to feed all the yarn on until you reach the bad section, then add or remove twist, for the length of the skein. The spindle does have one advantage – you can both put twist in underplied sections and take twist out of overplied sections in the same pass. On a wheel, you can only add twist or remove twist, so if your skein needs both, it would take two passes. You will want to wait for the skein to dry before respinning.

If you find your skein does not need improving, then go ahead and finish it as you had planned. Otherwise, re-ply it, then check again after its first soak.

The singles in a plied skein can't be altered at that point; they are what they are. A friend of mine edits out very thin spots or slubs as she crochets, leaving unworked lengths of yarn on the inside of her garment, breaking them and weaving them into the work when she is done. This solution works for knitting and weaving weft as well, giving you a final opportunity to improve the yarn or leave it in its as-spun condition.

## Navajo Ply

Navajo Ply is a chained yarn, with three side-by-side lengths of the same single. It is not a true three-ply, though it is often referred to as a three-ply. It does have a three-ply's characteristic roundness. The Navajo ply is a good way to preserve color changes clearly when spinning space-dyed roving, and to use up the entire length of a spindleful into a single skein.

To compare the strength of a three-ply with a Navajo ply, consider what might happen when one strand of the 3 strands is broken: in a three-ply, the other two strands maintain integrity of the length of the yarn; in a Navajo ply, the broken strand could potentially unravel and break the entire length of yarn, if the strands were to slide in the chain. A rough finishing of a Navajo ply skein can help reduce this risk.

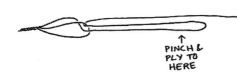

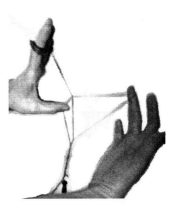

To start a Navajo ply, fold an initial length of your singles into thirds to make a leader for your plying spindle as you did with your two-strand ball. Keeping a finger in the loop at the other end of the length so it is kept open, ply up to that final loop. Now, draw a new length of the singles through that loop, maintaining tension between the single and the two strands of the loop, creating a new chain that can be plied.

This chain is the same style of chain used in crochet.

Efficient Navajo plying can be done on a spindle by making multiple chains, three or four, without plying, until the spindle reaches your feet, and then use a kick start to start the spindle. For a bottom-whorl spindle, the Peruvian hand roll could also be used to twist this pre-chained length.

I have not yet experimented with pre-chaining an entire ball to ply, similar to the two-strand ball – if you do, let me know how efficient you feel it is for you.

## A Full Spindle!

A spindle full of singles is ready to be prepared for plying.

Unwind the singles from the spindle. If you wound a beehive, you will be able to put the spindle whorl-down (top whorls are turned upside down, bottom whorls are right-side up) and feed off the end cleanly into a hand-wound ball. If you have two full spindles, they can be wound directly into a two-strand ball. If you have only one spindle, wind the first spindleful into a ball, then fill the spindle again and the second time, wind the first ball and the full spindle into a two-strand ball.

three Navajo chains

Or, slide the spindleful onto a straw or paper quill held onto the spindle shaft. This can be slid onto a lazy kate or a knitting needle for side-feed unwinding along with a second spindleful, into the plying ball. The kate is not a very portable solution, but the quill can always be taken along for winding on the go.

A spindle full of plied yarn, or singles to be kept as singles, is ready to be skeined and finished.

spindleful wound on niddy-noddy (photo by Iline)

With a beehive cop, you can put the spindle whorl-down and wind from the end into a skein using a skeiner, niddy-noddy, or appropriate body-noddy.

The skeiner is the least portable tool, so if you are on the go, pack along a niddy-noddy or use your arm or leg to wind the skein. The arm-noddy is good for an ounce or less of fiber; the leg-noddy works well with amounts from one to eight ounces.

If you are using a noddy, you can hold your tool in one hand and the spindle in the other, and wind around the noddy, regardless of how the cop was wound.

If you are a tool-hound, you could slide the plied cop onto a quill or straw, put it on a kate, and wind from the kate using a skeiner or niddy-noddy.

sliding cop onto straw (photo by sockpr0n)

Once you have a skein, use some waste yarn or break off lengths from the skein itself to put four evenly spaced figure-8 ties on the skein. They should be firm but not tight, so that water can move through the skein when it is washed.

Fill a sink with warm water and a little wool wash. Place the tied skein in the already filled sink for ten minutes. Don't agitate the skein in the sink; you can hold it under the water until it sinks on its own. Then, squish the skein for a minute or two to help it bloom. Squeeze the water from the skein, empty and refill the sink with cool water. Put the skein in, and squish it for a minute or two, then let it sit for five minutes. Squeeze the water from the skein.

contrasting ties on skein (photo by criminyjickets)

Underplied skein turns S, only once, so it won't bias. Overplied skein turns Z several times, it may bias when knit.

Wrap the skein in a towel and wring the skein out inside the towel, and then put into a dry towel to be whacked on the counter a few times. This lightly fulls the surface and helps the yarn to bloom. Hang the skein to dry. A balanced skein will hang in an open O. If it twists in the same direction as the ply, it is underplied; if it twists in the opposite direction to the ply, it is overplied. A skein can have up to two complete twists and still knit an unbiased fabric.

If your skein is singles, you can lay the skein on the counter in an O to dry for maximum bounce; it may have some pigtails occur in areas of high twist. Or, you may wish to weight the skein with a soup can while it hangs to dry, to block it open. Weavers block their yarns so that they will not stretch unexpectedly on the loom.

You may want to only gently finish your yarn, without squishing, using the same temperature wash and rinse water, and without whacking it on the counter — this will keep down the bloom of the yarn.

You may want to give your yarn a rougher finish — have a hot and a cold rinse bath, and move the skein between the two, squishing it roughly in each, until you feel the yarn constrict. The yarn will be lightly fulled by this treatment. When you whack it on the countertop, be very thorough to ensure the entire surface is fulled.

Whacking the skein on a countertop causes a light fulling of the surface and also brings out any halo of the fibers. If you do not want a halo in your fibers as yarn, you may wish to skip this step. Angora, for example, is easier to knit if not yet halo'd — it will halo as it is knit so you will not lose that lovely attribute of angora.

Once the skein is dry, sample and swatch for bloom (WPI) and drape (fabric). Wash your swatch as you would the finished item to accurately measure if you are getting the desired gauge or sett. Knitters and crocheters can make a four-inch or larger square. Weavers may want to make a small sample on a cardboard square.

spindle-spun skeins by mestina (photo by mestina)

**Productive Plying • 41**

# General Tips

## Transportability

A key to utilizing all available spindling time is to have your spindle with you. The safest container has stiff sides — tossing a spindle into a tote bag or backpack may lead to disappointment of the worst sort.

"Bruiser" was dropped and broken. Luckily, repair was possible. He returned home with a friend.

(photos by entrelac)

Ensure that your container has a sturdy lid or closure that will not come off accidentally — this is especially heartbreaking when the handle is in the lid and the container drops off while you are on the go.

A cardboard box with a flip-secure lid can be terrific secure storage inside a larger tote bag. A wine bottle container may even have a built-in rope handle, or you can drill holes in the sides of the container (not just the lid!) to add your own handle.

In addition to a sturdy container, consider how much time you will have to spin to bring along an appropriate amount of fiber. Also consider how many tools you may want to have with you — will you be hiking up the side of a mountain lugging everything, or are you travelling by car from stop to stop.

## Useful Tools

Tools can help your productivity, as long as they aren't stopping you from making progress due to their lack of portability while you're on the go. So, use them when you are at home base, but take advantage of the tools you have with you, no matter how minimal, to make progress on the go.

Knitting tote reused as spindle-carrier
(photo by bloomkitty)

A skeiner is the most efficient way to wind off a skein of yarn. The niddy-noddy is slightly more rudimentary, but portable; and for the lightest traveler, you have two niddies always available: the hand-elbow small niddy, and the longer knee-foot niddy.

A ball winder can be useful in preparing plying balls, though it will not wind as tight a ball as a hand-wound ball. It will give you a center-pull ball, if you desire plying a single spindleful: you can then hand-wind a two-strand ball from the ends of the center-pull ball.

skeiner and ballwinder (photo by marihana)

A nostepinne is more portable than a ball winder, and should let you wind a fairly tight ball. Check how tight the ball is once it is off the nostepinne, as a large diameter nostepinne may result in a loose ball. Once again, the nostepinne ball can be center-pull, so you could wind that and then hand-wind a two-strand ball from the ends of the center-pull ball.

A spinning water extractor is very handy for speeding drying time. This can be a washing machine (with the water turned OFF), a tabletop spinning almost-dryer found in RV accessory shops, or even a salad spinner. With none of these, you can wuzz a skein outdoors, swinging it in circles to drive the water out of it in a large spray.

A salad spinner gets water out of washed skeins.

## If you also Spin on a Wheel ...

If you also spin on a wheel, you may find that moving back and forth between the two improves both. Exploring new types of spinning – long draw, charka, true woolen, true worsted, novelty techniques allows you to see how versatile fiber is.

The spindler's typical stance of fiber in left hand and spindle in right hand mimics the traditional long draw spinner's stance where the right hand rotates the charka or great wheel and the left hand draws the fiber out. Wheel spinners may find handedness naturally switch to match the spindler's stance or long draw stance as you explore these techniques more.

As you sit at your wheel or twirl your spindle, consider your hand placement, both which hand is holding fiber and which is drafting, and how far apart your hands are. See if adjustments to match the other help or not.

If you have one, the level-wind flyer known as a WooLee Winder lets you focus on an even draft and on improving your spinning speed. Similarly, an electric wheel also lets you focus on an even draft, since it keeps the wheel at a steady speed.

Spinning wheel
(photo by riverpoet)

You may also find exploring additional fiber arts such as felting, weaving, nalbinding, embroidery, dyeing will add more to your fiber vocabulary and give you more insight into how fiber behaves.

## Spindling and Walking

When you spin at a wheel, your feet move. Spindling while walking is not such an insurmountable feat approached with that in mind.

I find bottom whorls are my favorite for this, perhaps because I can see all the yarn – or, because if it drops, the whorl hits first and my yarn is less likely to get dirty.

First – for portability – keep short pieces of fiber in your hand, and do your plying from a two-strand ball. Have a ready supply of more fiber – a wrist pouch, belt pouch, or secure across-the-shoulder tote bag. Yes, short pieces mean a lot of joins.

Then – see if a finger flick or thigh roll is for you. A high step for a horizontal thigh may work for you, try it and see. Flick at the thinnest point on the shaft for maximum oomph from your finger flick.

Spindling on the beach
(photo by himalaya)

As you walk, the spindle may sway. That's fine. It may even be fun or useful. Remember, the Peruvian butterfly brings the whorl in easy reach for wind-on.

General Tips ● 43

You'll need to develop your peripheral vision for tasks such as winding on while walking and drafting while walking. Keep to sidewalks and smooth surfaces in less crowded areas, or pathways you know well. You needn't stop while going up a staircase, as long as you are familiar with it.

What kind of walking?

Dog walking? Not so much. The dog needs your attention to his lead.

Exercise walking? Sure thing. The clip of a stiff walk may help keep your fingers twirling and drafting at a good pace! Strenuous hill climbing may need all your efforts, though, so try and see.

Slow moving lines – absolutely! The cinema, bank, post office, grocery – all have seen me with my spindles in my town.

Be safe – don't spindle while crossing the street. Look both ways!

Remember the kick start too, it can be a handy accompaniment to finger-flicking if a walking thigh roll isn't for you.

## Using Your Handspun

Spindlers have the ability to enjoy their fiber on the go. There are many ways to continue to enjoy your yarn once it is spun. For productivity, two considerations are how fast you can create a finished item with your yarn, and how much yarn the fabric will require.

knit spindle-spun hat by the husband of ellenspn (photo by ellenspn)

Between weaving, knitting, and crochet, in typical use, weaving uses the least amount of yarn, knitting is in the middle, and crochet uses the most. Of course, lace knitting or lace crochets may use less than weaving, and densely textured woven fabrics may use more than a simple crochet fabric.

Weaving is mostly a non-portable craft, though there are portable varieties with folding looms or small lap inkle looms. Knitting and crochet benefit from being as portable as spindling. So, you can craft a project from fiber to finished item all on the go with knitting or crochet, or spin on the go and weave at home.

It is the wraps per inch of your yarn that affects the gauge of crochet or knitting or sett of your weaving; the yarn density impacts the drape of your fabric.

yarn held double over needle gauge

A needle gauge can be used to choose an appropriate needle or hook for your yarn – lay two strands over the gauge, side by side. The hole that is completely filled by the two strands is the needle or hook size to use for a solid, not lacy or over-dense, fabric.

Knowing the needle or hook size lets you pick a published pattern to use your handspun for. Be sure to check drape in a knit or crocheted swatch to see if the drape will be suitable for the item.

Lace knitting typically uses fine yarn and a fairly large needle; fulled knitting and crochet use a needle or hook 3 or 4 sizes larger than the yarn would require for a solid fabric, so it makes a more open fabric suitable for fulling.

Spindle-spun, crocheted shawl by arielart
(photo by arielart)

Weaving sett depends on the fabric being woven — a plain weave uses a sett (ends per inch) that is half the wraps per inch for a solid, not lacey or over-dense, fabric, while twills and other multi-shaft patterns use a sett that is more than half the wraps per inch. There is a more complex calculation using the number of intersections of yarn that occur in a square inch, explained in weaving texts such as **The Weaver's Companion**.

Knowing the wraps per inch and determining appropriate sett for a given weaving draft lets you pick a published pattern for your handspun. Be sure to check drape in a woven sample to see if it will be suitable for the item.

Congratulations on creating wonderful spindle-spun yarns and items from them.

*Happy spindling!*

Tapestry woven landscape by breyerchic04 using commercial and spindle-spun yarns (photo by breyerchic04)

Hand-knit, hand-dyed spindle-spun wimple by chewiedox
(photo by chewiedox)

**General Tips • 45**

# Spindler's Bibliography

I can't guarantee you can find all these books -- many were out of print and second-hand when I got them. But they are all on *my* bookshelf amid the myriad more-than-spindle or other-than-spindle books, well-thumbed and referred to on my path to becoming the spindler I am today. New books are coming out on spindling as well, so I encourage you to look beyond this list.

**The Akha Spindle Workshop** by Wendy Whelan. A great pamphlet on spinning in the traditional way with the Akha spindle. No date, purchased in 2003 from Gemini Fibres.

**Gossamer Webs: The History and Techniques of Orenburg Lace Shawls** by Galina Khmeleva and Carol R. Noble (1998) has a section on Russian spindling, including their interesting plying method, from spindle to plying disc.

**The Handspindle ... Not Just For Demonstrations Anymore** by Paula J Vester (2002). A good pamphlet to learn with, nice photographs and concise text.

**A Handspindle Treasury: 20 Years of Spinning Wisdom from Spin-Off Magazine** by Interweave Press (2000). Selected articles on spindling from the first 20 years of Spin-Off. Many spindle tips, like quills for top whorls, as well as methods for tahkli, Akha, Russian, and Navajo spindles. A nice diverse collection.

**Handspindles** by Bette Hochberg (1977, 1980). The most amazing range of spindles from history, and in use today. A whole generation of wood-turners have been urged on by spindlers to re-create the Victorian silk spindle!

**Hand Spinning Cotton** by Olive and Harry Linder (1977). Covers almost all the tools to spin cotton -- Support spindle, bottom-whorl spindle, top-whorl spindle, Navajo spindle, charka, great wheel, and spinning wheel. (No mention of Akhas, though). Punis, natural dyes, and use of cotton yarns. Concisely thorough.

**How Nikki Shared Her Coat** by Detta Juusola (1994) a children's story with notes on collecting and spinning dog fur (factual part overlaps **Yes, It's Made from My Dog's Fur**, same author).

**Introducing Spindle Spinning** by Mike Halsey (1982) from scouring fleece, picking open locks to spin, to all the bottom whorling you can handle, singles and plies. Great sketches, thorough treatment of the material. I love the fact that it's clearly printed typewritten pages, too -- can't beat that typeface!

**Learn to Spin Cotton** from Cotton Clouds. Support spindle instructions included in their learn-to-spin-cotton kit. Nicely written. No date, purchased in 2002.

**Learn to Spin Cotton into Thread** A nicely diagrammed pamphlet of support spindle instructions, included in a kit purchased in 2002.

**Learn to Spin Silk on a Top-Whorl Spindle** by Ruth MacGregor (2002). A nice book on choosing a top-whorl spindle suitable for silk, silk types, and managing silk while spinning and plying.

**Learn to Spin With a Turkish Drop Spindle** by Wanda Jenkins (2004, 2008 with a DVD). Clearly written text and thorough photos walk you through learning to spin with a Turkish spindle. Includes the author's own wind-on for a great flat-bottomed ball of yarn. As of 2008, sold with a DVD too!

**Navajo Weaving Way: The Path from Fleece to Rug** by Noel Bennett & Tiana Bighorse (1997) has a nice section on Navajo spindle spinning (26 pages on the topic, from fleece to yarn).

**Russian Drop Spindle** from Peace Fleece. A short note about this spindle (a Turkish variant, not a Russian lace spindle) was included with the spindle. A nice little spindle, I enjoy mine! No date, purchased in 2002.

**Shuttle, Spindle and Dyepot** by Handweaver's Guild of America has spindling articles from time to time. I think they may have reprinted a collection too, but I didn't find that book on my shelf for compiling this list (darn it!)

**Simple Spinning on Sticks and Spindles** by Lionel Jacobson (1977). Gets you spindling from zero to the bottom-whorl spindle in no time. Plenty of sketches and rich in 1970's style. Touches on using the bottom whorl as a support spindle, too!

**Spin It: Making Yarn from Scratch** by Lee Raven (2003) a nice adaptation with new, color photographs, of the spindling portions of Lee Raven's earlier learn-to-spin book, **Hands on Spinning** (1987). Covers hand-carding, has some nice small handspun knitting projects in it, too.

**Spin Yarn on A Spindle** by Detta Juusola (1994) a thorough writeup of spindling, touching on collecting dog fur (which, granted, you are more likely to have on hand than a sheep in your back yard, if you're a city dweller!) Features her signature potato spindle and hangar niddy-noddy.

**Spin-Off Magazine** by Interweave Press, in particular the Spring 1995 issue with its focus on Handspindles. Many issues since **A Handspindle Treasury**, their 2000 compilation of past articles, also touch on spindling topics. Get your hands on a current copy to find out who peddles spindles online or in your area.

**Spin-Spin** by Heidi of My Paper Crane (no date, purchased in 2006). Covers top-whorl spindling, a little ungrammatical at times ... very current voice, I found it an interesting reflection on what the internet has done to open spindling to a wider audience.

**Spindle Spinning** (Needle Crafts 13 from Search Press) by Patricia Baines (1984). A nice, easy read geared to teaching the reader to spin primarily on a bottom-whorl spindle, with mention of hip spindles (see **A Handspindle Treasury** for an article on the topic of Lapland/Icelandic hip spindles) and support spindles as well.

**Spindle Spinning Cotton** by Patricia Baines (1994). A great pamphlet on the topic from picked cotton, making punis, to support spindles. Practical and clear. Has a useful discussion of charka spinning.

**Spindle Spinning: From Novice to Expert** by Connie Delaney (1998). Covers top whorl, bottom whorl, a note on Turkish, tahklis, and Navajo spindles. Connie Delaney also has pamphlets on Akhas, Russian, and Balkan spindles -- get them to round out her book (available on www.spindling.com). Her earlier pamphlet, Drop Spindling (1995), is completely covered in the book.

**Spindling: The Basics** by Amelia Garripoli (2003). For beginning spindlers, how to spin on a top-whorl spindle, with troubleshooting tips and further projects in fleece preparation and dyeing. (Yes, that would be my first spindling book!)

**Spinning In The Old Way** by Priscilla A. Gibson-Roberts (2006). A great update of her former (1998) book on the topic, **High Whorling**. Covers high-whorl spindles, with a mention of Salish (looks like a Navajo in the drawings) and Akha spindles. Covers fiber processing as well.

**Spinning With a Drop Spindle** by Carol Cassidy-Fayer (1997). Covers top- and bottom-whorl spindles. Not many drawings, but her website has some additional useful photos.

**Spinning With a Drop Spindle** by Christine Thresh (1971). A bottom-whorl spindling instruction book from raw fleece through plying.

**Spinning With a Turkish Drop Spindle** by Martha Moore (1996). Came with the Valkyrie Turkish spindle. A brief instruction pamphlet covering how to spindle in minimal words (very concise!) including winding on, that great mystery of Turkish spindles.

**Using a Navaho-Type Spindle** by Jan Symonds (1997) Covers the basic technique for spinning singles on a Navajo spindle. Great illustrations!

**Yes, It's Made From My Dog's Fur!** by Detta Juusola (1995). Covers fiber collection, preparation, and spinning from dog fur. Yay for our woofy friends!

Often, learn-to-spin kits are sold with pamphlets on spindling singles. Of the ones I've purchased, generally I find them readable and reasonably understandable: enough to get you started with singles, and itching to move on to plying.

Most books on wheel spinning may touch on spindling; **The Spinner's Companion**, for example, mentions spindle types. And Alden Amos's **Big Book of Handspinning** has several sections on spindle types (tahkli, top whorl, bottom whorl, Akha/Thai, Navajo /Southwestern), use, and even construction. Any book on fiber processing, textile history, and fiber types is as helpful to a spindler as it is to a wheel spinner.

Your learning need not stop at the printed word – there are also a *ton* of internet resources and forums for spindlers: Yahoo groups, Ravelry, YouTube, Flickr, blogs, websites, online magazines, online vendors and more.

## Accolades and Credits

This book would not have been as much fun without the great photographs contributed by Ravelry spindlers from the "Follow The Bellwether" and "Spindlers" groups. I only wish I could have taken photos from everyone who offered – limiting myself was tough! I hope you enjoy seeing not only my own spindles and spindling, but also that of other spindlers. It shows the breadth of top- and bottom-whorl spindles available, the range of spindle-spun yarns, and the use of spindle-spun yarn in a variety of arts and crafts.

The participants include (Ravelry name/real name): arielart/Arielle Finberg, artsyfish/ Joanne Fischer, bloomkitty/Mary K. Larson, breyerchic04/Sarah Townsend, chewiedox/ Diana Klau, criminyjickets/Dave Mackay, ellenspn/Ellen Bloomfield, entrelac/Ana C., leesy/Elise Cohen, lline/Line Lecerre, himalaya/Tracy Hudson, marihana/Mary Story, mestina/Kari, riverpoet/Tracey, sherie/Sherie McManaman, sockpr0n/Aija Goto, stringplayer/Barbara Ann Low, turtleknitter/Mary Hayne, wondermike/Mike Wade. Between them, wondermike and turtleknitter dreamed up the wonderful subtitle – I love it! It fully captures the spirit with which I wrote this book – the Now of Spindling!

It was my great good fortune that Joanne was willing to not only help with photo conversions to black & white but also give me advice and pointers as I tackled them too. Finally, I must give a big hug to Cathy Van Ruhan – she not only gave me the first golden nugget on my spinning path (staple length!) but her keen eye helped clarify many points and eradicate many glitches in early versions of this manuscript.

# Index

alpaca, 3, 24, 31
Andean plying ball, 22, 34
Andean plying bracelet, 8, 34, 36
angora, 3, 25, 41
balanced cop, 15, 25, 26, 27
balanced yarn, 8, 10, 30, 32, 37, 41
ball winder, 8, 42
batt, 31
beauty-wave plying, 37
beehive cop. *See* cop, beehive
bias, 10, 41
block, 41
bottom-whorl spindle, 1, 3, 11, 12, 13,
      14, 18, 19, 20, 21, 22, 27, 28,
      35, 40, 43, 46, 47, 48
cabled yarns, 32
camel, 25
cashmere, 3, 23, 25, 32
center weight, 15, 17
center-pull ball, 8, 9, 42
clockwise, 13, 14, 18, 19, 21, 32, 35,
      37
cop, 7, 12, 14, 15, 17, 18, 19, 20, 21,
      22, 23, 25, 26, 27, 28, 29, 34,
      35, 40
  beehive, 21, 22, 34, 40
  football, 21, 26
correcting yarn. *See* improving
cotton, 25, 46, 47
counter-clockwise, 5, 13, 19, 21, 32,
      35, 37
crepe yarn, 33
crimp, 3, 32
crimps per inch, 32
crochet, 9, 17, 29, 40, 44
drafting, 3, 4, 6, 8, 18, 23, 24, 25, 26,
      27, 30, 31, 32, 43, 44
  long staple, 24
  point of twist, 25
  short staple, 25
  spinning from the fold, 24
  woolen, 24
  worsted, 23
drafting triangle, 23, 24, 25, 27, 30
drafting web. *See* drafting triangle
ends per inch (EPI), 45
fiber diameter, 32
fiber hand, 5
fiber length. *See* staple length

finger flick, 15, 35, 43
finishing yarn, 9, 11, 37, 40
  rough-finish, 37, 39, 41
fleece, 3, 46, 47, 48
football cop. *See* cop, football
fulling yarn. *See* finishing yarn, rough-
      finish
gauge, 41, 44
guanaco, 33
gyroscope, 14, 15, 16
hand roll, 19
  Andean, 19
  Peruvian, 35, 40
high-whorl. *See also* top-whorl spindle
high-whorl spindle, 2, 47
hook, 12, 13, 15, 17, 18, 19, 20, 22,
      26, 28, 29, 38, 44
hook protectors, 28
improving
  plied yarn, 39
  singles, 38
  spinning speed, 43
  yarn as worked, 39
join, 7, 8, 24, 28, 29, 31
  felt (when plying), 38
  textbook, 7, 29, 30
  V, 31
  worsted, 31
join, 31
kate. *See* lazy kate
kick spin, 21, 35, 40, 44
knitting, 9, 17, 28, 29, 30, 32, 34, 38,
      39, 40, 44, 47
knitting needle, 21, 34
laceweight, 17, 25, 32
lark's head knot, 18, 19, 22, 35
lazy kate, 21, 26, 34, 40
leader, 5, 6, 8, 12, 15, 18, 19, 22, 25,
      26, 29, 35, 38, 39
lightweight spindle, 25
lizzy kate, 9, 33
longwools, 31
low-whorl spindle. *See* bottom-whorl
      spindle
merino, 32
mohair, 3
Navajo plying, 39, 40
needle gauge, 44
niddy-noddy, 9, 28, 40, 42, 47

nostepinne, 8, 42
notch, 5, 12, 19
overplied, 10, 32, 37, 38, 39, 41
pencil roving, 3
Peruvian butterfly, 19, 20, 22, 29, 35, 43
physics, 14, 21
ply, 2, 4, 8, 9, 10, 16, 17, 19, 21, 22, 23, 25, 28, 29, 30, 32, 34, 35, 36, 37, 38, 39, 40, 41, 42, 43, 46, 48
plyback, 8, 25, 30, 37
plying direction, 35
plying spindle, 16, 17, 39
predraft, 4, 31
production spindle, 25, 26
quill, 14, 26, 35, 36, 40
re-ply, 39
rim weight, 16, 17
roving, 3, 4, 5, 6, 7, 9, 12, 18, 24, 26, 28, 31, 39
S twist, 8, 9, 10, 13, 19, 21, 32, 35, 37, 50
sample, 8, 10, 30, 37, 41, 45
sett, 41, 44, 45
shaft, 12, 13, 14, 15, 16, 17, 18, 19, 20, 21, 22, 25, 26, 28, 35, 40, 43, 45
sheep breeds, 3
silk, 3, 23, 24, 29, 31, 46
singles, 16, 17, 19, 25, 28, 29, 30, 32, 34, 35, 37, 38, 39, 40, 41, 46, 48
skein, 9, 10, 30, 37, 39, 40, 41, 42, 43
skeiner, 39, 40, 42
slip-knot, 5, 35
snitch knot. *See* lark's head knot

spin direction, 13, 18, 32
spindle hand, 5
spindle kate, 21, 34
spit-splice, 38
staple length, 3, 4, 6, 7, 23, 24, 27, 28, 29, 30, 31, 48
thickness
    yarn, drafting, 2, 4, 6, 7, 24, 25, 29, 31, 32
thigh roll, 8, 9, 18
thigh spin, 14, 15, 16, 19, 20, 21, 35, 43, 44
three-ply, 32, 34, 39
top, 3
top-whorl spindle, 2, 3, 8, 12, 13, 14, 18, 20, 21, 22, 26, 27, 35, 40, 46, 47, 48
Turkish, 22, 23, 46, 47, 48
twist angle, 30, 38
twist direction, 5
twists per inch (TPI), 32, 38
two-ply, 25, 26, 27, 30, 32, 34
two-strand ball, 8, 22, 23, 34, 35, 36, 38, 39, 40, 42, 43
underplied, 10, 17, 35, 37, 38, 39, 41
vegetable matter (VM), 3, 26
weaving, 17, 20, 29, 30, 35, 39, 41, 43, 44, 45
wind-on direction, 5, 8, 18
wool, 2, 3, 9, 17, 23, 24, 25, 28, 31, 32, 40
woolen, 23, 24, 27, 31, 43
worsted, 23, 26, 27, 31, 43
wraps per inch (WPI), 17, 26, 32, 44, 45
yak, 25
Z twist, 4, 5, 8, 10, 13, 19, 21, 32, 35, 37

## About Amelia Garripoli ...

I began spinning on Mother's Day, 2001, with Lee Raven's **Hands On Spinning**, hooked stick, CD spindle, and Louet S-10. Since that fateful day, there was no holding me back; the spindles now overrun the bookcase and the wheels have formed a herd. I'm spinning the stash as fast as it jumps out of its cubbies, teaching and writing my discoveries for The Bellwether's fiber samplers and clubs, KnittySpin, Spin-Off, Yarn Magazine, and my blog, Ask The Bellwether.

I am "askthebellwether" on Ravelry, SpinOff, Knitty, and Flickr, and blog at AskTheBellwether.blogspot.com.
At home, I'm Amelia.

Amelia spindling a Crosspatch
fine wool/Tencel/bamboo blend
on a Forrester Dervish top-whorl spindle

50 ● **Productive Spindling**